NAVIGATING
YOUR CAREER

NAVIGATING YOUR CAREER:

TWENTY-ONE OF AMERICA'S LEADING HEADHUNTERS TELL YOU HOW IT'S DONE

CHRISTOPHER W. HUNT
&
SCOTT A. SCANLON
EDITORS

John Wiley & Sons, Inc.

New York · Chichester · Weinheim · Brisbane · Singapore · Toronto

Copyright © 1999 by Christopher W. Hunt & Scott A. Scanlon. All rights reserved.
Published by John Wiley & Sons, Inc.

Published simultaneously in Canada.

This publication is designed to provide accurate and authoritative information in regard to the subject matter covered. It is sold with the understanding that the publisher is not engaged in rendering professional services. If professional advice or other expert assistance is required, the services of a competent professional person should be sought.

Library of Congress Cataloging-in-Publication Data
Navigating your career : Twenty-one of America's leading headhunters tell you how it's done
/ Christopher W. Hunt & Scott A. Scanlon, editors.
    p. cm.
  Includes index.
  ISBN 0-471-25434-7 (pbk. : alk. paper)
  1. Career development—United States.   2. Executives—Recruiting—United States.
  3. Executive search firms.   I. Hunt, Christopher W.   II. Scanlon, Scott A.
HF5381.N358 1998
650.14—dc21   98-8157
                                                    CIP

Printed in the United States of America.

10 9 8 7 6 5 4 3 2

CONTENTS

Introduction   Christopher W. Hunt and Scott A. Scanlon   ix
About the Contributors   xi

Part I. Launching Your Job Search

1   Planning Your Job Search—How and When to Get Started   3
    David R. Peasback, Chairman and CEO,
    Canny, Bowen Inc.

2   How to Take Charge When a Headhunter Calls   13
    Smooch S. Reynolds, President,
    The Repovich-Reynolds Group

3   Interviewing with a Headhunter and Preparing for a
    Client Interview   23
    Dale Winston, Chairman and CEO,
    Battalia-Winston International

4   How to Target the Right Hiring Manager   35
    David H. Hoffmann, Chairman, DHR International

Part II. Hot Careers for the Next Millennium:
The Magnificent Seven

5   Wall Street: Land of Opportunity   45
    Brian M. Sullivan, President, Sullivan & Company

6   Information Technology   55
      Jeffrey E. Christian, President, Christian & Timbers

7   Consulting   65
      Charles W. Sweet, President,
      A.T. Kearney Executive Search

8   International   77
      Roderick C. Gow, Executive Vice President,
      LAI Ward Howell

9   Entrepreneurialism   87
      David Beirne, General Partner, Benchmark Capital

10 Entertainment/Media   97
      Gary Knisely, CEO, Johnson Smith & Knisely

11 Health Care   107
      Jordan M. Hadelman, Chairman and CEO,
      Witt/Kieffer, Ford, Hadelman & Lloyd

Part III. Plotting the Course

12 Big Corporation versus Small Company   123
      Paul R. Ray, Jr., President and CEO, Ray & Berndtson

13 A Ticket to the Top: What Functions Are the Power
      Bases to Senior-Level Management?   135
      Windle B. Priem, Vice Chairman and
      Chief Operating Officer, Korn/Ferry International

14 The Minority Candidate: Charting the Course
      for Men and Women of Color   147
      Herbert C. Smith, Chairman, H C Smith Ltd.

15 Returning as the Expatriate Executive   161
      Dwight E. Foster, Chairman, Foster Partners

Part IV. Now You're Sailing

16 Crossing Functional Lines   173
      Hobson Brown, Jr., President and CEO,
      Russell Reynolds Associates

17 A New Industry: The Transferability of Management
    Talent   183
        Gerard R. Roche, Chairman, Heidrick & Struggles

Part V. Reaching Your Destination

18 Evaluating the Job Offer   195
        Steven B. Potter, Managing Partner,
        Highland Search Group

19 Making Sense out of Dollars: How to Negotiate a
    Compensation Package   207
        John F. Johnson, Chairman, LAI Ward Howell

20 The Final Task: Integrating into Your New Company   217
        Gary S. Goldstein, President, The Whitney Group

21 So You Want to Be a Top Executive? Here's What It Takes   225
        Dennis C. Carey, Vice Chairman, Spencer Stuart, U.S.

    Index   235

INTRODUCTION

*Christopher W. Hunt
and Scott A. Scanlon
Editors*

It's an event that occurs thousands of times during the course of one's life-time—meeting someone for the first time. In almost every one of those encounters the question is asked, "What do you do for a living?" It is a question that is almost as common as asking the other person's name or noticing how tall they are or how they speak or walk. Indeed, an individual's occupation is one of the key measuring sticks by which we define or judge another person.

Managing your career or, more important, developing a career path that is right for you, is no longer a simple or easy task. In today's complex and volatile business environment, there is more than one path up the corporate ladder. We now view working at various jobs in different industries during the first few years of employment an acceptable route. This trial and error process is no longer regarded as evidence of a skittish or insecure nature but rather as a practical part of the learning curve that enables young professionals to weed out dislikes, identify roles in which they excel, and hone important business skills that they will need to build on later as their career develops.

Many young professionals, on the other hand, will have already addressed the career path issue by the time they have reached their mid-to-late 20s. Perhaps they were recruited directly from an Ivy League college or a topflight business school. These up-and-comers have carved out their career niche—

they are our future management consultants, investment bankers, or corporate lawyers. They are standing on the starting line of the fast track to senior management. Tomorrow's CEOs, chief operating officers, and presidents will be found in this fraternity.

Regardless of what early career path you are on, at some point your professional life will require change. Whether it is a small adjustment involving an internal shift from one department to another or a complete change in direction—perhaps even to a new functional discipline in a completely different industry in some foreign capital—you will need to know how to approach these transitions. How will you make the sound and rational decisions that are necessary when you reach that critical professional crossroads at age 38, 45, or 56? Even if you are on a secure management track, are there ways that you can improve your career or enhance your current position for an even more successful future at your company?

Navigating Your Career offers valuable insights and advice from 21 professionals who work at the cutting edge of a career management trend sector— executive search. Among the leaders in their industry, they have recruited some of the nation's highest-profile executives to major global corporations as well as to smaller, emerging growth companies that were in search of key leaders for the next century. They have been personally engaged in key trends which affect the growth and outcome of the careers of today's corporate professionals and have tracked, recruited, and advised many of these same executives over the course of their professional lives.

This book will cover all of the bases. From the early career-planning stages, these skilled search consultants will lead you through the interviewing and interfacing processes with recruiters and tell you how to appear on the radar screen of hiring managers within the corporate sector. The seven key industries of the new millennium are examined here, as are international career opportunities both from those looking outside the U.S. and returning expatriate executives. The nuts and bolts of managing your career are also covered in great detail, including how to negotiate the job offer and your compensation package, in addition to addressing the final stage in the career management process—integrating into your new company.

Career management is a decades-long process. However, if you approach this task with the right frame of mind, the proper attitude, and most important the best possible information, your professional transition and growth should be successful.

About the Contributors

David Beirne
Prior to joining Benchmark Capital as general partner in May 1997, David Beirne spent 10 years as managing partner of Ramsey/Beirne Associates, the leader in senior management, high-impact search for information technology companies. Mr. Beirne has developed a nationwide reputation for recruiting high-profile executives at some of the nation's largest IT companies, such as Microsoft, Netscape, and Novell.

Mr. Beirne holds a B.S. degree from Bryant College.

Hobson Brown Jr.
Hobson Brown Jr. is president and chief executive officer of Russell Reynolds Associates, Inc., the global executive recruiting firm. He specializes in the recruitment of chief executive officers and directors for clients in a range of industries.

Mr. Brown holds a B.A. in Economics from the University of North Carolina at Chapel Hill and an M.B.A. from The Wharton School, University of Pennsylvania.

Dennis C. Carey
Dennis C. Carey is vice chairman, Spencer Stuart, U.S., and co-managing director of the U.S. board services practice of Spencer Stuart. He specializes in the recruitment of corporate directors and CEOs for major U.S. corporations. He is also a member of the firm's high technology practice.

Dr. Carey holds a Ph.D. in Finance and Administration from the University of Maryland and was a post-doctoral fellow at Harvard University.

Jeffrey E. Christian
Jeffrey E. Christian founded Christian & Timbers in 1979 at the age of 23, thereby launching one of the pioneer firms in the executive search industry. Today he is widely recognized as one of the premier search consultants for major CEO assignments. In the past 19 years, he has impacted hundreds of

companies through his search practice, with clients ranging from young, fast-growth companies to major firms such as IBM, Adobe, Microsoft, Autodesk, Hewlett-Packard, and Apple Computer.

Dwight E. Foster

Dwight E. Foster is chairman and an executive managing director of D.E. Foster Partners Inc., which was formed in 1990 through a buy-out of the KMPG Peat Marwick executive search practice. He has worked extensively on U.S. senior management assignments for global companies headquartered outside the United States. Since the inception of Foster Partners, Mr. Foster has developed an international executive search delivery system with locations in 39 countries.

Mr. Foster received a B.A. in English from the University of Minnesota and an M.A. in Industrial Psychology at California State University.

Gary S. Goldstein

Gary S. Goldstein is president of The Whitney Group, a leading financial services executive search firm based in New York. Mr. Goldstein has extensive experience in human resources recruitment within all areas of the financial services industry. He has appeared in a number of printed articles and television programs, ranging from the *Wall Street Journal* to CNN's Moneyline, where he has discussed trends in the financial services sector.

Mr. Goldstein received a B.S. in Accounting and a B.A. in Psychology at Canisius College.

Roderick C. Gow

Roderick C. Gow is executive vice president for LAI Ward Howell. Mr. Gow has 15 years of executive search experience, with significant senior level recruiting in all areas of the financial services sector, ranging from investment and commercial banking to asset management and venture capital companies.

Mr. Gow received B.A. and M.A. degrees in Business Administration from Trinity College, Cambridge University.

Jordan M. Hadelman

Jordan M. Hadelman, chairman and CEO of Witt/Kieffer, Ford, Hadelman & Lloyd, has helped that company grow into one of the 10 largest executive search firms in the country. He has helped lead the firm's strategic diversification in health care and higher education to broaden the firm's penetration into managed care organizations, leading health systems and hospitals, physician group practices, Fortune 500 companies, and colleges and universities.

Mr. Hadelman received a B.S. in Business Administration from Georgetown University and an M.H.A. from George Washington University.

David H. Hoffmann

David H. Hoffmann is founder and chairman of DHR International. DHR, founded in 1989, is the ninth-largest executive search firm in the United States, with 41 offices across the country. A five-year growth rate of 351 percent makes it the fastest-growing of the top 10 U.S. search firms.

Mr. Hoffmann received a B.A. degree from Central Missouri State University.

John F. Johnson

John F. Johnson is chairman of LAI Ward Howell. He has 21 years of executive search experience focusing on boards of directors, chief executive officers, chief operating officers, and general management and human resources in the manufacturing and service industries.

Mr. Johnson earned a B.A. in Economics from Tufts University and an M.B.A. from Columbia University Graduate School of Business.

Gary Knisely

Gary Knisely is the chief executive officer of Johnson Smith & Knisely. During his 18 years with the firm, Mr. Knisely has conducted searches in a wide variety of industries, with a special emphasis on executive searches in the communications, entertainment, and media sectors. He has extensive experience in recruiting most business functions, particularly general managers, CFOs, and heads of marketing.

Mr. Knisely received a B.A. in Economics and History from Trinity College.

David R. Peasback

David R. Peasback joined Canny, Bowen Inc. as president and chief executive officer in 1988 after having spent fifteen years at Heidrick & Struggles, the last four of which were as chief executive officer of the firm and manager of its New York office.

Mr. Peasback holds a B.A. degree from Colgate University and an L.L.B. from the University of Virginia.

Steven B. Potter

Steven B. Potter is managing partner of the Highland Search Group. Before founding Highland Search, Mr. Potter headed the global banking and merchant banking practices at Russell Reynolds Associates. Mr. Potter specializes in senior management, corporate finance, investment banking products (high yield, M&A, restructuring), and leveraged buyout and direct investment assignments.

Mr. Potter is a graduate of Yale University.

Windle B. Priem

Windle B. Priem is vice chairman and chief operating officer of Korn/Ferry International, which includes 20 offices in the United States and Canada, and is also the head of global client services. Mr. Priem has 22 years of search experience and has recruited more than 80 presidents or chairmen for major financial institutions.

Mr. Priem received a B.S. degree from Worcester Polytechnic Institute and an M.B.A. from Babson Institute of Business Administration.

Paul R. Ray Jr.

Paul R. Ray Jr. is president and CEO of Ray & Berndtson. With 20 years of experience in executive search, Mr. Ray conducts search assignments at the board and senior management level. He was recently recognized for his outstanding contribution to the executive search consulting profession by being presented the Gardner W. Heidrick Award, the industry's highest honor.

Mr. Ray graduated from the University of Arkansas with a degree in business administration and holds a law degree from the University of Texas School of Law.

Smooch S. Reynolds

In 1987 Ms. Reynolds launched The Repovich-Reynolds Group (TRRG, Inc.) headquartered in Pasadena, California. The firm specializes in executive search with a special focus on senior investor relations, communications, and marketing executives for American corporations and major public relations consultancies.

Ms. Reynolds holds a B.A. degree in Broadcast Journalism from the University of Southern California.

Gerard R. Roche

Gerard R. Roche is chairman of the international search firm of Heidrick & Struggles. During more than 30 years as an executive recruiter, Mr. Roche has worked with hundreds of corporations and their corporate boards. He has placed more CEOs than any other recruiter at companies such as IBM, Eastman Kodak, CBS, PPG, Polaroid, AT&T, and Allied Signal.

Mr. Roche received a B.S. from the University of Scranton, an M.B.A. from New York University, and an Honorary Doctor of Laws degree from the University of Scranton.

Herbert C. Smith

Herbert C. Smith, Ph.D. is the founder and chairman of H C Smith Ltd., an executive search firm located in Shaker Heights, Ohio. He has over 25 years of recruiting experience, and in 1985 established a firm through which he has represented companies and organizations recruiting middle to senior and board level professionals.

Dr. Smith is a graduate of George Williams College, earned an M.A. from the University of Chicago, and a Ph.D. from the University of Pittsburgh.

Brian M. Sullivan

Brian M. Sullivan is president of Sullivan & Company, a retained executive search firm serving clients in the global financial services marketplace. Mr. Sullivan founded Sullivan & Company in 1988, and by 1998 the firm had grown to become one of the largest in the United States. Mr. Sullivan recruits senior financial services executives, ranging from CEOs of investment management firms to heads of divisions for major global investment banks.

Mr. Sullivan received a B.S. degree in Finance from Lehigh University and an M.B.A. in Finance from Denver University.

Charles W. Sweet

Charles W. Sweet is president of A.T. Kearney Executive Search, the executive recruiting division of A.T. Kearney, Inc., a global management consulting firm, which is a wholly owned subsidiary of EDS. In his search career he has personally completed more than 500 search assignments covering virtually every functional area in a wide variety of industries.

Mr. Sweet earned a B.A. degree in English and Economics at Hamilton College and an M.B.A. in Personnel and Finance from the University of Chicago.

Dale Winston

Dale Winston is chairman and CEO of Battalia Winston International, a New York–based executive search firm with a 35-year history. Ms. Winston is nationally recognized in the human resources field for her work in executive search, management development, and organizational planning. Her valued opinion is often sought by prominent news sources such as *The Wall Street Journal*, *U.S. News and World Report*, WCBS News, and CNN.

Ms. Winston is a board member and chairs the Communication Committee of the AESC. She received a B.A. in Psychology from Finch College.

I

LAUNCHING YOUR JOB SEARCH

PLANNING YOUR JOB SEARCH— HOW AND WHEN TO GET STARTED

David R. Peasback, Chairman and CEO,
Canny, Bowen Inc.

PLANNING YOUR JOB SEARCH—
HOW AND WHEN TO GET STARTED

David R. Peasback, Chairman and CEO,
Canny, Bowen Inc.

In today's volatile and unpredictable business environment, perhaps only one thing is certain: Change is a constant. As companies try to cope with the relentless pressure to deliver improving profits year after year, the newspapers continue to be filled with reports of the latest megamergers, downsizings and changes in senior management. And with the steady stream of technological innovations and heightened global competition, the pace of change is accelerating. Sweeping organizational changes have even become part of the recent history of what used to be the most stable and paternalistic of American companies, such as AT&T, Eastman Kodak, and IBM. On an individual basis, executives can no longer realistically expect to retire from the same company where they began their careers. In fact, during the course of their professional lives, most people will work for several different organizations—and often in more than one industry.

Having accepted the inevitability of change, the question then becomes how to best prepare for it. "Change management" has become one of the trendy catchphrases of the 1990s—and, when it comes to your career, you must be your own change manager. At crucial points throughout the various stages of your career, you must decide if and when it is time to move on. When that time does arrive, you can take proactive steps to make the transition to your next company as expeditious and painless as possible.

There are many different circumstances under which people change jobs. Ideally, the decision is voluntary and self-motivated, such as when an individual is recruited away for a better opportunity. Increasingly, however, the change is involuntary and unexpected, as in the case of a corporate restructuring, consolidation, or when a company determines that it is more cost-effective to outsource a given function. As companies constantly try to reinvent themselves to become more productive and profitable, more and more executives are being confronted by the prospect of an involuntary job change.

Although companies have become more cooperative in helping terminated employees find new employment (such as offering outplacement assistance and writing letters of recommendation), the conventional wisdom is that it is always better to look for a new job while still employed. We concur with this philosophy. We reject the argument that it is necessary to devote full time and attention to the search for a new position, and that, therefore, a person should leave his or her current employer to do so. First, it is always better to negotiate from a position of strength. Second, despite the fact that employers know, intellectually at least, that in today's market more qualified people than ever are unemployed through no fault of their own, from a psychological standpoint employers want to believe they are luring away someone who is indispensable. Even if an executive has the most legitimate of reasons, corroborated by references, for leaving his or her last company, some residue of doubt remains in the mind of the next prospective employer. The belief that there might be more to the story often lingers on. Finally, if you engage in a search when your current position is still secure, you are likely to project more confidence and be more discriminating in deciding upon your next affiliation.

Recognizing the Warning Signs

Consequently, it is important to pick up on the warning signs, both internal and external, that indicate it is time to move on. What then are the telltale signs? There are a number of key questions the professional must ask. First and foremost is, "Am I happy?" Whether you are a recent college graduate, a middle manager, or a senior executive, job satisfaction should be viewed not as icing on the cake but as a basic requirement. Obviously, during periods of economic decline, one may sometimes have to grin and bear it until conditions improve. Keep in mind, however, that even during severe recessions companies continue to initiate searches for qualified executives, and new opportunities develop at all levels.

In the tight labor market we have experienced during recent years, with the national unemployment rate hovering at around 5 percent, there is no excuse to stagnate in an unfulfilling job. If you are unhappy in your present position, your discontent will almost certainly manifest itself in your performance and attitude.

A related question is, "Am I still learning and developing?" If your job has become repetitious and stale, and offers little or no opportunity to broaden your skills, it may be time to initiate a search. Sometimes, of course, it is possible to transfer to another, more challenging position within the same company. But in the absence of this alternative, it may be necessary to jump-start your career by switching functions or industries, or joining a company in the same industry that does a better job of organizational development, or finding one where there are simply more opportunities.

In terms of marketability, the importance of continuously upgrading and expanding your skills cannot be overstated. Leading-edge companies—those that consistently outperform the competition and which tend to be the most selective in their recruiting process—place a premium on job candidates having a wide range of experience. It is for these reasons that, particularly early in your career, it is advisable to obtain international experience and, still more important, cross-functional experience. If you aspire to become a chief financial officer, seek opportunities in marketing or operations. If you are on a marketing track, be receptive to veering off for a stint in financial planning and/or running a shift in the plant. If your ultimate goal is general management, obtain experience in as many functional disciplines as possible. Acquiring experience in new-business development and in turnaround situations is also highly valued by today's most discriminating employers. Because rapid and constant change has become so intrinsic to doing business today, flexibility itself is regarded as a core competency.

Generally speaking, the clients we deal with today are placing an ever greater value on diversity of experience. Over the last ten years, we have observed nearly a complete reversal in our clients' perception of job moves. A degree of stability is still important, but when we present a candidate who has remained with one company for the duration of his or her career, our client is now likely to express concern that the person's thinking and management style have become too inbred. Prospective employers question how effective such a person can be if moved into a different environment and culture. At the same time, clients have become somewhat more tolerant of frequent job moves, especially of those made early in one's career. Job-hopping is still frowned upon, but with the average company tenure now being about five years, clients are more likely to perceive an unsuccessful one-or-two-year stint at a company as a broadening experience and as a sign that the individual is willing to take risks. These issues will be addressed more fully in following chapters, but suffice it to say that you should never stop learning—and that when developmental opportunities cease to exist, it may be time to move on.

Other warning signs that it is time to contemplate a change require less soul searching and are more obvious. If, for example, you are being passed over for promotions, are receiving mediocre performance reviews, and are being awarded only nominal raises and bonuses, it is hard to miss the writing on the wall. The same can be said if you find yourself out of the information-and-decision-making loop. In other cases, particularly at more senior levels where there are fewer avenues of advancement, it is simply a matter of being blocked by people of similar age at similar points in their careers. The management log-jam at successful organizations like General Electric has generated chief executive officers for countless other companies. In other cases still, you may find that you simply have no chemistry with your boss. Assessing the personal chemistry fit between our clients and candidates is undoubtedly the most critical and challenging aspect of conducting executive search assignments.

Up to this point, we have discussed reasons for changing jobs that have to do with job fulfillment and how you stack up and are regarded within your company. But what if the problem is with your company *itself?* Perhaps you are even on a fast track—but in a company that is going nowhere. The products your firm makes or the services it offers are being supplanted by a new technology. Or your company's market share is steadily eroding and its reputation diminishing. Perhaps all of the resources in your company are being poured into another division with higher growth potential. These conditions are also valid reasons for commencing a job search.

There are other warning signs that register at the corporate level. If your company is acquired, your position may become immediately vulnerable as economies of scale are realized. Depending upon your position, even if your company enters into a merger of equals, you may find yourself in competition for your own job, as no company requires two chief information officers, two vice presidents of communications, or two general counsels. Often, of course, merger announcements come without warning. But if you are in an industry that is going through massive consolidation, such as regional banking or rail transportation, you would be well advised to explore possible contingency plans.

Even in the absence of a merger, changes in senior management, in particular at the CEO level, have become more common. And on innumerable occasions, we have seen the arrival of a new CEO followed by a broad revamping of senior management. Frequently, a new CEO will bring in his or her own team, even if the incumbents are perfectly capable. Once this process begins, there is often a trickle-down effect.

Laying the Groundwork for Your Search

There are certain practices that a forward-thinking executive should adopt, as a matter of routine, even before seriously considering a job change. First, we urge you to maintain a current resume. As recently as five to ten years go, recruiters would look with some suspicion on an individual they approached who offered to fax or mail an updated resume on little or no notice. This was a possible red flag, indicating that the individual was perhaps on shaky ground in his or her present company or perhaps already engaged in an active, if discreet, job search. But with all of the turmoil in corporate life over the last several years, recruiters are now more likely to view the maintaining of a current resume as nothing more than simple prudence and common sense. And because recruiters may be working under tremendous time pressures in trying to fill the search, they will appreciate a readily available summary of your background and accomplishments, rather than having to painstakingly cover all of this information in an extended telephone conversation. In the initial telephone screen, the recruiter's objective is to establish whether there is a preliminary fit—a fit "on paper" if you will—between a prospective candidate's background and a given search. If the apparent fit exists (and, of course, provided there is mutual interest), the details of your background can be filled out in a face-to-face interview.

Second, when a recruiter calls, always accept the call. Because an executive recruiter is proffering this advice, it may sound self-serving. We realize that many busy executives, particularly those in hot areas like high technology, are inundated by calls from recruiters. Nevertheless, for a variety of reasons, it is wise to make time for the call. Even if the position the recruiter is currently describing is of no interest to you, speaking to him or her can provide a prime networking opportunity. In being helpful by suggesting colleagues, friends, or others who might have an interest in the position, you accomplish several desirable goals. Provided that your recommendations are thoughtful and on target, you will elicit the gratitude of the individuals you referred. (If you think of someone who is not actively in the job market and you are uncertain whether or not the person will appreciate you mentioning his or her name, you can always call that person, describe the opportunity, and pass along the recruiter's name.) People will be grateful that you made the effort and will be likely to reciprocate when you are in the market or when they hear of an opportunity that seems well-suited to you. At the same time, the recruiter will not forget your helpfulness. At the very least, spending a few minutes talking with a recruiter is a good opportunity to exchange market intelligence.

Networking should not be limited to establishing relationships with executive recruiters. It is a good idea to be active with the relevant industry associations. Similarly, writing articles for trade publications and participating, either as a speaker or an attendee, in industry conferences and seminars go a long way toward increasing your visibility. In conducting research on a search assignment, recruiters zero in on the names of people who are quoted in or compose articles for trade journals, or who appear on the attendee lists of seminars. Furthermore, attending a conference is an excellent way of meeting the people who are catalysts and decision-makers in a given industry or function. It is not an exaggeration to say that, in many instances, the substantive content of conferences is really just an excuse for holding a grand-scale networking/social event.

Personal networks should not be neglected, either. Belonging to charitable organizations, doing volunteer work, even attending parties and dinners can put you in contact with individuals who are predisposed to helping you and who, someday, may indeed do so.

Most of the strategies we have discussed should be employed before, during, and after a search for a new job. Once you have successfully landed a job, it is a good idea to send letters of acknowledgment to the individuals who played a role, no matter how fleeting, in your search. In so doing, you are not only thanking people but also accomplishing the dual objective of informing them of your new affiliation.

How to Make Your Exit

Part of preserving your network upon changing employers is knowing how to exit gracefully from your previous job. It is obviously foolish to burn your bridges behind you. And if you conduct yourself in an above-board, professional manner, you may even be able to reinforce your bridges. As recruiters, we find that some of our most prolific and reliable sources of leads for prospective candidates are their former employers.

In making a graceful exit, it is important not only to give proper notice, but also to depart as quickly as possible after conferring with your manager. In an exit interview, you should be forthcoming about the nature of your new job. If you can be constructive and tactful, you may also be in a position to offer advice to your boss that would have been awkward or impossible to convey under normal working circumstances. Obviously, respect the intellectual property of your former employer. Also, do not disparage your former company and coworkers to customers, recruiters, or others. When people ask why you left, try to phrase your answer in a forward-thinking, positive manner, rather than launching into a critique of your former company.

Changing jobs can be a stressful, sometimes even traumatic, experience. But this transition process also provides opportunities to forge lasting and meaningful relationships and to refine interpersonal skills that will serve you well in other facets of your career. Because macroeconomic and organizational changes are occurring at an ever more feverish pace, you will have to approach change within your own career differently than in the past. By expecting the unexpected, learning to spot warning signs, and continuously cultivating your network, you can manage change to your ultimate advantage.

2

HOW TO TAKE CHARGE
WHEN A HEADHUNTER CALLS

Smooch S. Reynolds, President,
The Repovich-Reynolds Group

How to Take Charge When a Headhunter Calls

Smooch S. Reynolds, President, The Repovich-Reynolds Group

The best rule to follow: Return that call, return that call, return that call.
The second best rule: Be helpful and responsive, be helpful and responsive, and be helpful and responsive.

The Reality of a Recruiter's Call

In today's highly competitive marketplace, truly exceptional talent is a scarce commodity. And, with the increasing demand for top-notch professionals, recruiters are delving deeper and deeper into organizations to identify talent. As a result, the likelihood of your being approached and courted by a recruiter has increased dramatically in the past few years.

From the inception of the executive search profession, a high degree of mystery has swirled around the notion of what executive recruiters are and do, not to mention how they actually discover you, the Candidate! So, let's strip the mystery from the scenario, and focus on the fundamentals of responding to any recruiter who may contact you. After all, the next such call you receive may be the very one that serves as a catalyst for catapulting your career to new heights!

Taking Charge When the Recruiter Makes an Overture

If you've never dealt with a recruiter, don't let the seeming awkwardness of not really understanding much about what we do (or what it is that we want from you) turn you into a reluctant participant. As noted in the previous chapter, remember that whether you are gainfully employed and content (perhaps thriving) in your current position, or seriously contemplating a job change, it will be to your advantage to accept the recruiter's call. *View it as an opportunity—not an annoyance.* Consider the call a chance to develop and build a relationship with an individual whose livelihood will, hopefully, bring you your *best next* career move.

If you have dealt with recruiters before, you probably have countless questions about whether interfacing with them is actually a benefit or a hindrance. You are also probably wondering why the recruitment community has so many styles, approaches, and expectations in its dealings with professionals.

So, let's address the most critical issue up front: Most recruiters are interested in engaging a prospective candidate in an earnest conversation that will enable them to become more familiar with that individual's career, and with his or her future career intentions. As a result, nearly every call and every interaction that you have with a recruiter can be beneficial to you in either the near term or the long term.

Dual Roles of the Professional Contacted

Critical to the success of your relationship with a recruiter is to recognize that as the professional being contacted by a search firm, you serve in a dual capacity—as a potential candidate for a specific position, and/or as a source of other candidates for that position. Regardless of which role you serve in, your positive interaction with an executive search professional will be one of the smartest survival strategies available in today's competitive marketplace.

Taking charge in this relationship can mean a variety of things to both sides of the equation. On your side, when a recruiter calls, you should be prompt in responding and demonstrate some interest in engaging in an open, free-flowing exchange of thoughts and ideas. The conversation should explore everything from inquiring about the recruiter's firm (especially if it is an unknown one to you), to learning more about the recruiter's own background and experience in the executive search arena, to listening thoughtfully to the details of his or her current search.

In most instances, a recruiter will be calling to inquire whether you are interested in a specific search that he or she is conducting. Some calls may pique your interest, and others may not. The most important factor to remember is that you must convey to the search professional *precisely* what your career aspirations are, and aren't. To accomplish that, you should take charge and outline your own parameters and limitations as a candidate without being concerned that there will be any negative repercussions at all. You *must* be candid and communicate directly and honestly. With this posture on your part, the relationship will evolve into one that is truly meaningful to both you and the search professional.

Should you decide that the opportunity that the recruiter has described is not for you, don't feel sheepish about indicating that it is not quite what you believe would be your best next career step. More important, take advantage of the opportunity to shift your role in the relationship. At this point in the conversation you now have the potential to become, in the mind of the recruiter, a valuable source of candidates for his or her search. As a result, listen even more carefully to the specific details about the position, and volunteer to refer professionals who you deem highly qualified for that particular position.

The Value the Professional Derives beyond Serving as a Candidate

Now, let's address that very subject of referring candidates. Remember, everything that you say and do will reflect significantly on the recruiter's perception of your value as a source of candidates—and, more significantly, on his or her perception of you in general as a professional. Consequently, make sure that you do not recommend individuals of mediocre talent, or who only meet a few of the recruiter's criteria for the position. Only mention those you consider as *"best in class"* within your specific profession. A recruiter would much rather that you not refer any candidates than to have you recommend ones that will only waste his or her time. Poor referrals reflect negatively on your evaluative skills and your ability to make sound, objective judgment calls.

Developing the Relationship

Taking charge also applies to how you shape the relationship into the future. Will you wait until the recruiter needs you, or only call when you need the recruiter? Or will you occasionally contact the recruiter to keep him or her apprised of new developments in your career, and possible new career interests on your part? Experience has shown that to maintain a relationship, you need to keep a recruiter informed, "engaged," and interested in you as a professional, on a continuing basis. Making your conversations meaningful can include educating him or her about trends you see in your functional specialty or within your specific profession or industry.

I think it is important to acknowledge that the executive search profession is comprised of as wide a variety of mindsets, approaches, and styles of individuals as any other profession. Some are more straightforward in their approach and recruitment style, and others simply are not. *However*, remember, short of a recruiter displaying unethical or unprofessional behavior, *it is in your best interest* to have a free flowing exchange of thoughts and ideas with members of our profession.

Benefits to the Professional

Many professionals will ask, is this process really all that beneficial to me? There are really two parts to this discussion: (1) the literal, short-term benefits of the search process, and (2) the less-tangible, long-term benefits of developing and evolving a relationship with a recruiter. Both of these components of executive search are exceedingly beneficial to you, if you leverage the opportunity to begin and nurture a relationship with an executive search professional. The reasons are numerous, but here are a few that should remain at the top of your mind:

- *Marketplace value.*   Conversations with recruiters often are quite revealing about the compensation value/price tag that a professional/ function may have. This type of information could be of tremendous importance to you as you examine your own value to your current employer against peers within your company for the purpose of defending peer equity issues with management, and within both your specific profession and industry.
- *Marketplace intelligence/Trends in industries and functions.*   Recruiters are the professionals closest to the heartbeat of global corporations when it comes to industry expectations, and future trends that senior management worldwide will be embracing in the next millennium. Oftentimes we are privy to information that the rest of the world isn't

necessarily involved in prior to a company effecting a particular strategy. We serve as excellent benchmarking figures and resources about these issues. And, we rely on professionals like yourself who are immersed in myriad corporate functions to provide us with much of the rudimentary knowledge that enables us to counsel our clients on how to frame and redefine a position/function. In addition, this information also allows us to predict, to a reasonable degree, what the future of corporations worldwide may look like.

- *Career navigation/networking.*   As executive search professionals, we are in the business of assisting executives in the rethinking and the navigating of their career strategies. Indeed, when we approach you, a new career strategy and plan may not yet be top of mind; however, as you interact more and more frequently with us, we can often assist you in reshaping your career in ways that you never thought possible. Equally as important, even though you may be content in your present position, the recruiter may be working on a search assignment that could provide your next best career step. Or, the recruiter may share an opportunity with you that could result in your career taking a completely different and refreshing course. Networking and building credible relationships with executive search professionals can be the best catalyst to career moves that most professionals never even contemplate.

So, the moral of the story (at least as it pertains to the benefits for you as the professional being courted) is to never underrate the value of a recruiter's call.

When Should You Call a Recruiter?

Finally, when and how do you recognize that fateful moment in time when you should make the call to the recruiter? There are basically two choices in this matter: (1) wait until you are desperate to leave your current position, or (2) take a proactive approach and build solid relationships with your recruitment contacts *long before you need them.*

Waiting until you are completely dissatisfied with your current job is not the wisest way to navigate a relationship with an executive search professional. When layoffs are impending at your company, or a colleague gets the promotion that you thought you had earned, or your department's budget gets slashed by 50 percent, you should *not* wait until you're ready to quit before you think about developing a relationship with the executive search community. (If you *have* waited until that point, bide your time and develop some solid relationships with recruiters before you share the totality of your frustrations!)

Similarly, the notion of throwing oneself into every search that comes your way can result in the same loss in credibility with the recruitment profession. Both of these approaches undermine your credibility. The first approach puts you in the compromising position of having to lower your expectations about the quality of the opportunity that you consider, because you are so desperately unhappy in your current situation. The second (shopping the possibilities, if you will) positions you as a professional who is indecisive, possibly looking to leverage another company's potential interest in your talent as a means of either validating your own worth, or as a means to garnering higher compensation with your current employer via the threat of taking another position. *Neither* of these approaches will gain you anything. In fact, you will lose credibility with the executive search community, and eventually the calls from recruiters will stop coming.

One of the most important things to remember is that as recruiters, we are constantly evaluating professionals' frames of mind. Our clients retain us to determine the mindset of all of the professionals whom we deem qualified for a specific position. Given that premise, remember that your mindset when you interact with a recruiter is critical to the relationship that you will develop and evolve with us.

The most important advice that I can offer you is to be proactive, engage in a two-way exchange of thoughts and ideas, and don't wait until your present position becomes tenuous or untenable before you approach the executive search community.

Baring One's Soul

One of the difficult decisions the professional has to make when navigating his or her career is deciding how much information to share with a recruiter. In this instance as in others, one of the old-fashioned adages is still the most applicable today: honesty is the best policy. Be candid, direct, honest, and professional in your dealings with the executive search community, and this will result in the most effective and productive relationship for both you and the executive search professional.

Presenting Yourself in a Credible Manner

Understanding how the executive search profession defines its community of professionals deemed worthy of contacting (otherwise known as the "radar screen") is exceedingly difficult. In reality, there is no commonality or consistency from one search firm to another in terms of who qualifies to be on the radar screen and who is not. As a result, the process of distinguishing oneself with the recruitment profession has become, oftentimes, an overwhelming task to contemplate. However, in my view, one overriding factor will set apart any professional as far as career navigation is concerned and as far as "making it" onto the radar screens of small and large search firms. It's simple. Focus on *best practice* in every contribution that you make in your current position, in your overall profession, and in the counsel that you provide to your subordinates, peers, and senior management. All of these will culminate in making you a professional who deserves to be considered for new and challenging career opportunities.

Interviewing with a Headhunter and Preparing for a Client Interview

Dale Winston, Chairman and CEO,
Battalia-Winston International

3

Interviewing with a Headhunter and Preparing for a Client Interview

Dale Winston, Chairman and CEO, Battalia-Winston International

You are comfortably settled in your 23rd-floor corner office, enjoying the unobstructed view to the south, when your secretary announces that an internationally known executive recruiter is on the phone. Should you spend valuable time discussing career opportunities when you are perfectly content where you are? The answer—as you already know from reading Chapters 1 and 2 of this book—is an emphatic "Yes," of course! What may not yet be clear, however, is that there also is much to be gained by moving on to the next steps in the job-transition process—engaging in face-to-face interviews with search consultants, and even with potential employers— even if a career move is the farthest thing from your mind.

Here is why. First, I have found over the years that it is important to periodically take stock of your career, no matter how happy you are with your current situation. As part of this self-assessment, you will want to ascertain how marketable your skills are—and recruiter and client interviews will provide you with valuable career marketability feedback. Second, it is helpful to develop and maintain relationships with recruiters just to hear about potential opportunities. Third, you should accept the opportunity for engaging in interviews at least every year or two just for the sake of practice. I have had candidates who have spent all of their careers with one company, and, ironically, they have been harmed by their lack of interviewing experience. Clearly, if a job opportunity is not interesting to you, a client interview may not be worth your while. But, if the job is within a certain "range," it is healthy to try to do an interview, even if you are really happy where you are. It's rather like the old story of selling a business that "no one wants to sell—but at a certain price, some will."

Preparing for the Interview with the Recruiter

Once you have made the decision to accept a recruiter interview, there is always the potential that this particular job opening could be the ideal opportunity for you. Therefore, it is very important to do your homework and be prepared. Ask the consultant to send you material on the company. Research it on the Internet. Request the job specification so that you know how to focus your skills and background. More than likely the recruiter will ask you for a resume (every senior executive should have an updated resume). If you don't already have one, this will stimulate you to put one together. More important, the recruiter might actually help you evaluate it.

The Interview with the Recruiter

Each recruiting consultant typically has a different style of interviewing, and it is important that you be sensitive to the dynamics of the individual to whom you are presenting yourself. Recognize the pace of both the interview and the interviewer. If the style of the interviewer is sharp, crisp, and to the point, don't start wandering off with irrelevant details. When the interviewer is interested in those details, he or she will ask for them. If your background is highly technical, understand that the recruiter is there to evaluate your experience and career development. It is up to the client to evaluate your technical capabilities.

The recruiter will most certainly ask you to describe your background. Don't be shy. This is your opportunity to highlight your accomplishments. Be precise and explain how you contributed to the specific results. Even though we work in a team-style delayered environment today, you need to distinguish between the "we" and "I" in your answers. How are you part of a group, and what is your individual contribution to that group? There is a delicate balance. Be prepared to give examples of the process you went through to achieve your accomplishments.

Another focus during your recruiter interview ought to be on communicating your strengths to the consultant. Rather than stating a laundry list of perceived strengths, it would behoove you to describe situations in which your strengths were utilized in actual events. If your strength is to be a participative manager, motivating teams to function effectively, you are a good facilitator. Hammer this home. If your strengths lie in fast-paced management change, make that the primary theme of the interview. If you indicate your strengths through your actions properly, the interviewer will never have to ask you point-blank "what are your strengths?"

Be results-oriented. You want to be prepared to give some quantitative results of your accomplishments. Even the most qualitative of functions can have quantitative results. The vice-president of human resources might have reduced turnover by X percent, or was responsible for overseeing benefits cost containment. Be honest about your areas of weakness or need for personal development. Reflect upon your most recent performance review and its relationship to your career development. You should have some ready answers. One of the classic (and maybe best) responses to "what are your weaknesses?" is "I am impatient." You are being honest about a weakness, but you are couching it in a diplomatic way.

Obviously, you will need to share information with the recruiter that is relevant to your background and skills. However, if you are being considered for a position with a direct competitor of your current employer and you possess certain proprietary information about strategic plans or new products, you certainly do not want to share that. The recruiter is clearly not there to perform industrial espionage, and should be very respectful of your judgment. If the interviewer asks too many detailed questions about matters you deem proprietary, simply explain that you are not at liberty to discuss such matters.

The recruiter may ask you for some personal information—questions about your background or inquiries regarding what is important to you as an individual. A good executive search consultant will have a solid understanding of the culture and value system of the client organization, and he or she will want to analyze your personal style and value systems to see if they are a cultural fit. It has been proven that one of the key requirements for people to be successful in a new assignment is that they share similar values with the organization they are joining.

One of the things you might do before you agree to an interview is check with the Association of Executive Search Consultants, or with Hunt-Scanlon to determine the credibility of the search firm. Many of the credible firms are members of the Association or listed with Hunt-Scanlon, although certainly not all.

I have found over the years that professionals generally make career moves for one or more of three reasons:

1. *The potential the job offers.* It is important that you share with the recruiter your short-term goals, your long-term goals, and how they may or may not be realized in your current organization. From that information, the consultant can determine whether this could be the right opportunity for you.

2. *The people.* A good recruiter will be familiar with his client and will know the style of the people who are successful in that organization. So, again, be willing to share information about your background, and your likes and dislikes so that the recruiter can get a sense of whether you'll mesh with the client.

3. *The money.* You should be honest about your compensation package. Immediate or near-term compensation adjustments are of course important, but you also might choose to move because you recognize the long-range rather than short-range benefits to be realized. There are times in professionals' careers when it may be worth making a lateral move because of long-term opportunities.

Finally, it is very important to share with your recruiter any personal information that he/she might not feel comfortable asking you about, but which you feel might have an impact on the position. Tell the recruiter about your family. If your spouse works, you have certain additional family responsibilities. You want to volunteer information that might influence a relocation or a significant change of lifestyle.

One caveat: If the client interview is about a job that requires relocating and you are adamant about staying in a particular location, decline the interview and do not waste the recruiter's and your time.

Preparing for the First Client Interview

One of the things you want to accomplish during your meeting with the search consultant is to really get a sense of the person with whom you will be meeting in your client interview. You want to find out what to expect from the interview process. Your first interview might be only with the client's hiring manager. The hiring manager may be in charge of all first interviews.

There are a number of different models. Obviously, the more information you can gather about the people you will be meeting, the more prepared you will be. The more research you do about the company, the more knowledgeable you will appear. They will be impressed with your diligence.

Here are some of the ways you can prepare:

1. If the client is a public company, ask for an annual report from the search consultant.
2. Seek out the client's web site or access "the financials" from EDGAR (SEC web site).
3. Locate and review recent articles that have been written about the company, so that you might ask knowledgeable questions, such as "I saw that you were exploring a merger with XYZ company three months ago. Is that still being considered?"
4. If the company is a large one, try to find someone you know who works there or has in the past. Recognizing the confidentiality of the situation, you may look to them for more background information.

We often get calls from people we have known over the years (it is good to have headhunters as friends!), saying "I'm going to interview at XYZ Company—Do you know anything about them?" They know that we respect confidentiality and can help.

During the course of your research, you will uncover information that might cause you to be more or less interested in the opportunity. If the information excites you, share that point. If the information you develop causes you concern, go back to the search consultant before you meet with the client and explain that "I'm reading this or I'm hearing this and I'm not sure it's right." Do not go to the client directly with your concerns.

What to Wear to the Interview

Men

When it comes to interviews, there are no "Casual Fridays." Normally, I would recommend a blue suit for a man, but that depends on the company conducting the interview. In other words, if you are interviewing for an entertainment company in Los Angeles, you don't need a blue suit, but you should wear a suit. Don't let the "laid-back" atmosphere influence your choice of attire. Even at IBM, where the dress code currently is casual, you cannot be overdressed for an interview. This policy, by the way, applies to your interview with the executive recruiter as well. The recruiter is your first screen. So—blue suit, white shirt, and a tie. It need not be a conservative tie: after all, ties are a reflection of your personality. So don't run out and buy an "interviewing tie." Wear something you like that reflects your own style. The suit can be double-breasted, or it can be European. Wear to an interview what you would to a business dinner. And wear conservative brown or black shoes.

Women

Women should always wear a suit to an interview, preferably one with a skirt, not pants, and preferably in a subdued color, although that can depend upon the time of year. But I wouldn't wear a pink suit or a red jacket to an interview. Stockings should be skin-toned and sheer. Basically, your interview dress should reflect your style, but not make a statement. You can wear jewelry or pearls, but not five bangle bracelets that rattle and clang during the course of the interview. This is the time to look neat and proper, and have your clothing almost blend into the background so that your professionalism is what is noticed. When I finish interviewing a woman, I want to walk away with the feeling that I didn't notice what she was wearing.

Grooming

A woman came to the office today for an interview, and it was obvious that she had just come from the hairdresser. Well, I thought that was good—I would probably have done the same. A fresh haircut is a good idea for both men and women. As far as a man's beard is concerned, if you wear one, you wear one. However, we once had a bearded gentleman who was an excellent candidate for a food company, but they took issue with his beard.

If you are traveling to an interview, take along an extra shirt or an extra top. Be prepared. Take clothes fresh out of the cleaner's bag. Some years ago, during a very hot summer, we interviewed a man who had flown in from New Orleans for the day. By the time he had arrived at our office in a taxi with no air conditioning, his shirt was literally soaked. He was going directly to an interview with a major bank in New York. We deliberately finished our interview a little early so he could go to Brooks Brothers to pick up another dress shirt before his interview.

What to Bring to the Interview

Candidates who arrive armed with notes and information on the client company (perhaps a printout of their web page) impress me. I am further impressed when they bring a list of questions. When an interview is about to conclude, the search consultant usually asks, "Do you have any questions for me?" If a candidate whips out a paper with a list of questions and begins to check them off, one by one, saying, "Well, you covered that, and you covered that," as opposed to "No, I don't have any questions," it is more positive. It demonstrates that the candidate is organized and has given the interview some serious thought. The fact that I've covered everything on their list is fine. And, often it can prompt a candidate to ask me a question that hasn't been covered. It is a good idea to bring along relevant materials such as a client's annual report, web page, and so forth. You may not use them, but having them available will give you a psychological edge.

Where Do We Go from Here?

After the interview, be sure to follow up with a note or a phone call to the recruiter thanking him/her for their time and informing them of your level of interest in the opportunity. Having had the time to assess your interview with the executive search consultant, it's very important for you to give him or her your reaction to the particular opening. Use this opportunity to develop a relationship with the recruiter. If you are not interested in the opportunity, perhaps you might suggest the names of other individuals who might be appropriate. Be sure to let the recruiter know when you are interested; however, be respectful of his/her judgment as to whether you are appropriate for the assignment. If they feel there is not a fit, conclude by establishing an open line of communication for the next opportunity that becomes available, when the fit may be more appropriate.

Preparing for the Second Round of Interviews

After you have gone through your first round of client interviews, you will find that the second round can take many different directions. While the first interview might have required that you meet with the senior management team, the second might find you meeting the hiring manager and spending more time. Or the first interview might have involved the hiring manager and maybe a human resources executive, and the second interview can now involve the rest of the team. Our world today is "delayered," and decisions are typically no longer made in a hierarchical fashion, so they take much longer. As a result of the restructuring that has occurred in corporate America, often many people will participate in the hiring decision. It used to be that a manager alone recruited you to a team—today the whole team participates.

Typically, you can expect to meet 3 to 5 people. But I have seen instances where candidates meet as many as 20. They don't all necessarily have decision-making powers, but they do have a voice. Your recruiter can probably tell you at the outset exactly what the process is going to be.

Another thing you might want to ascertain is what stage the client is in the course of the search. Are you the first candidate—or the sixth one? If you are the first, you're kind of a pathfinder, while if you're the sixth they may be measuring you and your answers against others. How has the search been organized? Some clients simply like to see a flow of people; others like to see a final slate. Understand that if you interview early on in the process, it is going to take longer. On the other hand, if you are a later entry, you might have less of a window in which to make a decision.

Preparing for the Final Interview

Keep in mind that in the first and second interview stages you are selling. Never forget that although you are learning about the organization, you cannot turn down a job until it is offered. It is that third and final interview when you know that they are interested, and now it is your turn to ask the questions and to have them answered. The more a candidate learns about a company, the position, and the environment, the greater the likelihood of making a wise career decision. I have had candidates who, once they have gotten to that final stage of interviewing, ask to meet their potential subordinates so as to get an even better understanding of the work environment and the team.

Frequently the final interview for senior positions might be accompanied by dinner with spouses. A lot of diligence goes into senior-level hiring. The interview process is not just one of evaluating skills, management potential, and visionary potential; it is also a process of getting to know one another so that people will place themselves in environments in which they are compatible and, therefore, can succeed. There is no generic talent for success. I don't know anyone who can be successful in every environment. It is a style issue. Your style and your skill-set, no matter how good you are, have to meld into the style of that organization.

How Can I Be Sure the Interview Will Be Kept Discreet?

Ensuring that a job interview is kept discreet is a serious issue with most executives. This is where the due diligence you have done around the executive search firm you are working with will be very important. If you make it clear to the search firm that you are in no way on the job market, and that you have *not* initiated the process yourself, they will be very sensitive to maintaining discretion. In my position, I work with a lot of CEOs. Since they come from a variety of different companies, discretion is even more difficult to maintain. We limit their exposure in the early stages of a search by working strictly with a company's search committee, often comprised of several members of a board, rather than the entire board. This way discretion is kept around the long list of candidates who are being spoken to before we expose some candidates to the full board. Typically, if you are at middle management level or even at senior management level, you are dealing with highly sophisticated people who don't want to expose you. So, for example, when we are working with a candidate at an early referencing stage, we will try to get the names of people with whom they used to work who are no longer at the same company, just to ensure discretion.

It is incumbent upon the candidates themselves to remind the consultant and the client company that they are not on the market. You as the candidate need to ask your search consultant at what point in the process you might be in jeopardy of being exposed. The consultant should be able to pinpoint this for you. If, during the process, someone in your company does hear that your name is out there, you can always slough it off. There is really nothing mutinous about looking around. And, as always, the best defense is a good offense: "If I didn't get calls, then you really wouldn't want me, would you!"

How to Target the Right Hiring Manager

David H. Hoffmann, Chairman, DHR International

How to Target the Right Hiring Manager

David H. Hoffmann, Chairman, DHR International

Finding and making the right career moves rank among life's most important decisions. These pivotal changes generally occur only four or five times during one's lifetime, and they clearly define who we are and what we're all about. Locating the right hiring manager can be a critical factor in this career-advancing process, but like the maze of lines on a road map, there can be many different routes to the ultimate destination. Success, however, almost always involves paying attention to several key components. Effective networking and achieving a high level of visibility are two of these components. There are several obvious ways of doing both that should be explored and utilized. Trade associations, organizations, and fraternities that relate to your field of expertise and employment are excellent sources for contacts. Be sure to establish and nurture relationships with executive search firms. Get active in social organizations, your church, school, and youth athletic activities, to name a few—and don't pass up opportunities for public speaking engagements that will put you in the limelight. In short . . . be visible!

When and How Does One Make the Approach?

My answer is simple. Upon learning of a potential opportunity, if the timing is right, and if the proper groundwork has been laid as outlined above, your ability to stay on top of potential opportunities and to pursue them will be a very natural evolution. Quite often through thorough networking and maintaining of visibility the approach will come to you instead of the other way around.

Always keep in mind that you will never be too early or too forward if you approach an opportunity yourself. Persistence pays off. I recommend a two-pronged approach to ensure success. When dealing with executive search firms, for instance, it is wise to write and call someone in the research department as well as one of the firm's senior-level consultants. Major search firms are inundated with solicited and unsolicited resumes every day. For example, at the Chicago office of DHR International, where our firm is headquartered, the daily mail arrives in boxes that may contain as many as 500 resumes! It is quite possible to get lost in the shuffle, so a little extra effort can pay dividends.

This same approach should be used when dealing directly with a potential employer as well. No one will be offended if, in addition to sending a letter to the Human Resources Department, you also write to the department head of the area you are targeting, and to the chief executive officer or chief operating officer as well if you feel it is appropriate. When preparing to call, try to get the individual's direct line. If your path in isn't clearly mapped out, write first and then follow up with a direct telephone call. Keep in mind that in today's world of secretarial screening (that is, if you're lucky enough to hear a real voice) and voice mail, the time of day when you call is critical. I recommend calling generally between 5:15 and 6:15 in the afternoon. Frequently, the executive at this time of day is reviewing and retrieving his messages and voice mails and has a tendency to pick up the phone personally. This is an effective tactic that we at DHR International have used to speed up our own search process.

It is important to keep in mind that executive recruiters and company hiring managers are not intentionally unresponsive or lax in answering requests for interviews or in returning telephone calls. It is simply a case of having to prioritize their time and the demands that restrict these individuals. This problem of accessibility is the single most important reason that an entire chapter in this book has been devoted to targeting the right hiring manager.

How Do You Get Your Foot in the Door?

Almost any tactic that will get the hiring manager's attention will be a plus; however, the professional must not get so creative that it appears that he or she is being devious. I recall an individual who had learned of a search being conducted by our firm, and by me personally, for a chief operating officer position. This person called me to set up an appointment to meet, under the pretense that he was a chief operating officer of a European-based corporation. He told me that his company was planning to move its headquarters to Chicago and was in need of several senior-level executives. Thirty minutes into our discussion, the individual finally confessed that his call was simply a ploy to get in to see me personally, because he really wanted a shot at the COO opportunity but had experienced a history of unanswered phone calls and inquiries to search firms. The simple fact was that I found his deception to be appalling, and he was immediately crossed off our slate of potential candidates. With the exception of this character flaw, his resume actually looked somewhat promising for the opportunity.

The best way to get one's foot in the door is to be very accomplished and professional at what you do. A sterling reputation, both within and outside of one's company, is typically what brings candidates to a potential employer's or an executive search firm's attention. When I am engaged by a client company to conduct an executive search, some of the first questions I ask are: "How do you feel about your competition? Do you know of any individuals within competing industries that you may want us to target? Are there any professionals that you have been impressed with at any related trade associations, clubs, or industry meetings?" During these discussions several names will typically surface. When search firms dissect their client companies' competition, referrals are often made by members already within the client companies—and often they derive from contacts and relationships that have been formed through trade or industry associations.

Be Concise and to the Point in Your Resume!

Be aware that four- and five-page unsolicited resumes get lost in the paper shuffle. *Concise* one-page summaries with highlighted, bulleted significant accomplishments are the real attention getters that attract search firms and hiring managers alike. These people encounter literally hundreds of resumes that require sorting and reviewing. Stand out—be different and unique! And through it all *never lie about anything on your resume*. The truth always prevails!

What Is the Best Entry Point at a Target Company?

Always include the human resources department or representative when making inquiries into a company. Human resources personnel generally have the best handle on the complete staffing needs of an organization. Moreover, they often are deeply involved in any hiring or termination discussions. But I also recommend targeting a senior executive, as well as a supervisor in your specific function or discipline. They, too, have definite business plans and knowledge of promotions, terminations, and departures that are on the radar screens—but which may not yet have surfaced or been communicated throughout the organization.

How to Find Out That a Job Opening Exists

Build relationships with executive search firms. Through the newspaper, learn which companies are hiring. Attend trade seminars to become knowledgeable about trends within your particular industry. Use your network!

Seeking a Position within Your Own Company

The best way to gain serious consideration for a promotion within your own company is to do an outstanding job in your present position. Be a leader when internal committees or meetings are conducted. Take on added responsibilities whenever the situation presents itself or the need arises. Communicate your career goals and ambitions to your superior, especially during performance evaluations. Be a good mentor to subordinates. At DHR International, we have a policy that simply states no one can be promoted until he or she has successfully groomed and mentored his or her successor. This puts pressure on the business to create opportunities and to be constantly looking internally for promotional opportunities. At the same time it ensures a certain degree of continuity and stability to the company.

A Final Word on Gaining Visibility

Get to know the leaders in your industry. Start at the top and build personal relationships. Get acquainted with your peers in competing companies to open up and establish channels for continued networking. Write articles for trade journals. Getting published in a related trade magazine or publication will give you exposure and can open up career opportunities.

This attempt to give the reader an inside track at targeting the right hiring manager can only outline a strategy. With the advent of electronic resume scanners and other highly advanced technological developments employed by various companies, the entire targeting process can at times become frustrating if not overwhelming. Try to keep in mind, however, that ultimately there will be faces and personalities involved, and use this current technology to your advantage. The "getting known" factor is becoming easier in this marketplace full of opportunities.

HOT CAREERS FOR THE NEXT MILLENNIUM: THE MAGNIFICENT SEVEN

WALL STREET: LAND OF OPPORTUNITY

Brian M. Sullivan, President, Sullivan & Company

5

WALL STREET: LAND OF OPPORTUNITY

Brian M. Sullivan, President, Sullivan & Company

Wall Street has always offered a wide-open career track with significant financial rewards for the bold and adventurous, for those with great ambition and the ability to think big, and for those possessing the nerve to make huge bets and take large positions. Until very recently, however, Wall Street was not noted for strong management techniques and philosophies. But as old-style partnerships have given way to modern financial institutions with global reach, scale, and public ownership structures, strong management cultures have evolved that place a premium on what has become the most important asset on Wall Street today—intellectual capital. Therefore, there has been more emphasis on finding tomorrow's superstars.

Today there exists on Wall Street a broader and deeper career track than ever before, and as a result it is attracting a broad cross section of the best and the brightest talent in the country and the world. It is, perhaps, the business world's most exciting working environment—precisely because of the talented people who are drawn there.

This chapter will address why career opportunities are so attractive on Wall Street, list the skill and education requirements for entry, and pinpoint the personal attributes that are crucial to success. For the purposes of this discussion, we will use *Financial Services* and *Wall Street* synonymously to mean the activities taking place in financial institutions around the country. These include the corporate finance, research, and advisory activities of the "sell side"—institutions that help corporations raise money and sell securities to institutions and individuals—as well as the research, portfolio management, and marketing activities of the "buy-side" institutions, firms that manage investments for institutional investors, mutual funds, and high net-worth individuals.

Also, there will be some general career navigation advice for students charting a course toward Wall Street, as well as for the seasoned executive contemplating a midcareer change in that direction.

An Opportunistic Environment

Wall Street is, perhaps, the most competitive environment in business today; certainly it attracts people who thrive on competition. There is no such concept as coming in second on Wall Street—winning is everything. It is truly an environment where only the top tier survive.

- If you don't evolve and you don't keep moving forward, you perish.
- If you don't adapt to changing conditions, you cease to exist.
- If you don't specialize, you become obsolete.

Although Wall Street is not a jungle, it possesses many of the same characteristics. Given that, why should it be so attractive to so many talented individuals? The first reason is opportunity to gain responsibility. More than in other industries, people are judged upon their knowledge of an industry, an historical trend, a new mathematical valuation methodology, or a creative approach to financial engineering—all of which may have been accumulated during a course of academic study. Overall, there are few "dues" that need to be paid on Wall Street. If someone has a good idea that creates a competitive edge, that person will be welcomed.

On the sell side, helping your client (usually the CEO or the CFO) means improving shareholder value through various financial management techniques—managing to earnings expectations, maximizing assets, raising capital, or making strategic acquisitions or divestitures, to name a few. Success depends upon sweat equity and intellectual capital—long hours and hard work, coupled with specialized knowledge and creative thinking. On the buy side, serving your clients can mean challenging conventional thinking on valuation processes, being able to spot an emerging industry sector that the rest of "the street" has not yet identified, or building relationships with counter-parties that provide better access to buy or sell on your terms in front of the competition.

A second reason for Wall Street's lure is the opportunity to create your own market value. Once you have been trained on the sell side and have selected a specialty—be it investment banking, trading, sales, research, or mergers and acquisitions advisory work—you are effectively running your own business. You may operate as part of a team, but at the same time you are developing a franchise that consists of *your* specialized knowledge, *your* contacts, and *your* track record. It's the same on the buy side: your proprietary value grows in proportion to your knowledge and experience. In effect, you can run your own show while using someone else's capital to build your own franchise.

A third reason is opportunity. Wall Street is a meritocracy. At one time securities firms formed an exclusive club in which membership was limited to an "Old Boys" network. While there were opportunities for those without college educations, they were limited. There were no women, except in administrative supporting roles, and few if any minorities. Today that has changed. Wall Street has an enormous appetite for talent and it is blind to background, color, gender, and religion.

A fourth reason is excitement. Wall Street is a dynamic environment that is constantly reinventing itself. It is fast moving—time frames are measured in hours, not days or months. Along with telecommunications, technology, transportation, and pharmaceuticals, finance is one of the few sectors that is truly global. Finance is an international language; the world's markets are so interconnected that a currency problem in Asia or a political problem in Latin America can cause a chain reaction in far-flung financial markets and affect trading on a grand scale. It is an environment in which information is the ultimate strategic weapon. Insights on a planned change in tax policy or the direction of interest rates can translate into millions of dollars.

Finally, Wall Street is the epitome of capitalism. It touches every aspect of our society and every business in that society, whether large or small. It is concerned with institutions and individuals from "cradle to grave." It exists solely for one purpose—the formation of capital. In that way, the environment is brutally straightforward and honest. Wall Street is not dedicated to any altruism other than creating value that can be leveraged into wealth.

What It Takes: Skills and Education

Wall Street is an industry based on specialization. Success is achieved by the application of high intellectual power, laser-like focus, and specialized interests. Thus, the sooner a professional can become a specialist, the sooner he or she can begin developing a knowledge base upon which to build a power base. On the sell side, that means settling on a functional specialty (e.g., investment banking, sales and trading, research, marketing, or derivative pricing). On the buy side, there are similar options: portfolio management, financial modeling, marketing or relationship management. These are the first of many such choices: Next the professional focuses on an industry sector, and then, in some cases, a geographic area (such as Latin America or Eastern Europe).

Until the 1980s Wall Street prized generalists; today the exact opposite is true. As opposed to industries that promote cross-training and horizontal integration, the key to success on Wall Street is to develop and refine an area of specialized interest and to build upon it by adding incremental doses of knowledge and experience.

For younger people in college or graduate school who are planning a career on Wall Street, there is a need to master a technical discipline. For executives already in the workforce who are considering a career move to Wall Street, that requires identifying an area of specialized knowledge or experience that can quickly be converted in revenue-generating ideas.

It is fair to say that an MBA degree is required for those entering Wall Street today, although other advanced degrees are present there, as well. Mathematical academics are prevalent in certain specialized areas, including risk management, new-product development in derivatives, and debt instruments. Regardless of the nature of the degree, however, technical expertise is a base requirement.

Beyond educational degrees, there are other credentials that will serve the professional well. A general requirement is the facility for effective communication and the art of persuasion. Whether you're on the buy or the sell side, success hinges on an ability to influence people through a clear and coherent explanation of ideas. There are many failed financial products and instruments that could have been successful—had they been properly launched and marketed persuasively.

The same advice on specialization applies to those who want to switch to Wall Street from another career or industry. If you possess a specialized knowledge base or particular experiences or skill sets that can be converted into revenue-generating products or services, you may be able to make the transition. The deciding factor is whether your specialization can be transformed into revenues. A CFO in a particular industry, for example, might be able to become an equity research analyst if he or she knows enough about the industry and the major competitors.

The Right Stuff: Attributes and Attitudes

Wall Street's sell side is structured like a pyramid, with a base composed of thousands of eager, bright young graduates who are willing to work 85 to 100 hours per week to learn the business. This is a demanding environment that requires energy and, more important, endurance and persistence. Responsiveness is measured in minutes and hours, and no cost in personal effort is too high to win or satisfy the client.

On the buy side, different characteristics are evident—most notably patience, skepticism, and an attention to detail. No investment decision is to be made until all the pertinent information can be unearthed, analyzed, compared, and tested. Like the sell side, the buy side requires tremendous amounts of work and analysis, even though the outputs are different.

Neither environment is a comfortable one for someone looking for regular, steady work of the 9-to-5 variety. Wall Street requires tireless dedication and great personal sacrifice. Some Wall Street professionals rationalize the enormous commitment of time and energy on the basis of the rewards to be realized; others just see it as part of the job.

It is true that there are not many graybeards on Wall Street. Whether that is the result of the long hours and exhausting working conditions, or because successful players make enough to retire at a young age, the fact remains that working on Wall Street is physically and emotionally demanding. Those who survive and prosper are those who are basically entrepreneurial, singularly dedicated to succeeding, and willing to take chances. Chance may take the form of willingness to experiment and fail, or a willingness to work hard for low pay in order to learn a business and develop a specialty.

Inventiveness is another desirable attribute. New products are introduced every week on Wall Street, but many of them are just variations on a theme—new ways of looking at or improving upon an existing product concept. Still others are brand-new concepts, like strippable coupons on bonds, or convertible securities. Who knows what Bill Gates might have come up with had he not started Microsoft with Paul Allen? My guess is that he would have developed artificial intelligence software to manage some sophisticated derivatives trading.

A final thought on personal attributes before moving on: Although it's dangerous to generalize, I believe that many successful Wall Street professionals display an independent streak. Wall Street players may exhibit herd-like behaviors, but there is a good deal of contrarian thinking, too. The independence is a question of the chicken or the egg coming first: Having a solid client following and a strong revenue base can contribute to a professional's spirit of independence, but it is also true that Wall Street attracts self-confident people with clear goals, focus, and determination.

Career Advice: Setting the Right Course

If your profile fits the preceding description, Wall Street might be the right place for you. The next step is to find out.

Getting Started

If you are a student, it is important that you determine as early as possible what your specific interest is and try to formulate a course of study that will advance your knowledge of that area as well as your marketable skills. Special projects or term papers should be used as opportunities to develop an expertise. Quite often, these opportunities can be converted into an interview and can become the substantive component of the decision to hire. The next step is to secure a summer job or internship in your chosen specialty area. This may help you get a job upon graduation and will boost your market value—which can be in important differentiation in today's buyer's market.

If you are a recent graduate or just entering the workforce, it is important just to get in the door and to develop some experience. The key is to find an area of specialization that appeals to you and plays to your skills and inclinations.

If you are making a career change, the route to Wall Street may be not so direct, but the goal is still attainable. Chances are that it will require some concession on your part, such as a pay cut. Again, it is a buyer's market, and the competition among the best and brightest young people for positions is fierce. So, you've got to prove your worth all over again. On Wall Street, people have no value until they can create value.

The good news for you is that nearly everyone starts out on the bottom rung and has to work their way up. There are very few shortcuts to the top, and there is no substitute for the value of generating revenues. One strategy to convince people that you have specialized knowledge is to write an analysis of a particular company or industry with which you are familiar, pointing out the areas for exploitation and growth while analyzing inherent weaknesses. *The competition is everyone else. Your goal is to show that you have value that can be turned into revenue.*

Networking is an important step in the process of getting your first Wall Street job. Talk to professors or friends and neighbors who work in finance. Contact security analysts and journalists who cover the industry, to get their opinions. If you have difficulty making these calls, that's a clue that you don't have the drive to make it on Wall Street.

Moving Up

Once you land a position on Wall Street, be concerned about becoming an expert. The keys to moving up are simple, straightforward—and difficult to execute:

1. Become an expert. Develop a niche. Create specialized knowledge that can be converted into a service or product.
2. Cultivate contacts and develop a following. Begin developing a profile associated with your niche and your contact base.
3. Find ways to generate revenue. You will never be taken seriously on Wall Street until you control client contacts and produce revenues. On the buy side, revenues come from adding incremental assets under management (marketing) and performance fees (portfolio management).
4. Increase your revenues and advance up the food chain. Having a revenue flow also makes you attractive to other firms who want to build their bottom line with your contacts. Thus, you don't have to start at an elite firm—you can always move to one with your clients.
5. Don't sit still—keep moving forward. Add continually to your knowledge base, your skill base, and your client list. Expand your expertise to related areas.

6. Maintain your edge. Don't be afraid to take calculated risks if they can appreciably improve your position. The same applies to job offers. Don't fear changing companies, providing that such a move gives you a better platform for your product or service and your client base. If you were running a Fortune 500 company, you would spend a significant amount of time trying to understand the competition. Learn what competitors are doing. Find out who their clients are and what products or services they are providing. Never stop learning.

7. Stay focused on clients. Clients are your reason for being.

To the Millennium and Beyond

It is impossible to predict with certainty what the future will hold. One thing is certain, however. The competition on Wall Street will continue to escalate. As a result, new ways of thinking, creative problem solving, and fresh talent will always be sought after and embraced.

INFORMATION TECHNOLOGY

Jeffrey E. Christian, President, Christian & Timbers

6

INFORMATION TECHNOLOGY

Jeffrey E. Christian, President, Christian & Timbers

Information technology is making careers. The activity involving individual wealth creation in information technology and the growth of new information technology businesses will soon dwarf the activity of any other industry of the last 100 years—including automotive manufacturing, computers, semiconductors, electricity, oil, gas, and entertainment. The information technology marketplace is becoming an increasingly significant piece of the gross national product. If you are striving to become a player in this marketplace, you have several choices to make in order to bring yourself into the mainstream spotlight.

Information technology now drives the economy, increases workforce productivity, lowers distribution costs, and plays an integral role in every industry from consumer products to manufacturing. It used to be something found primarily in the Northern California Silicon Valley area and used only by "IT types," but today information technology touches everyone, from those in the schoolroom to those in the boardroom. If you are not using e-mail, you are behind the pack. If you do not understand what an Internet community is, you are behind the times. And if you are not figuring out how to use e-commerce in your business, you will be behind your competitors.

This unlimited potential and growth brings a new challenge to CEOs and business managers. Leaders not only need to keep up with new technologies and evolving business practices; they need to focus on the competition and assess their own position in relation to these other established companies. Today, competition in the information technology space can include a future company that is being funded tomorrow and is not yet in business today. The rules of the game have changed and the rules of engagements have changed. In order to win in this game, you must set a precedent and create and follow the constantly changing rules.

Starting Out in Information Technology

The information technology industry is experiencing some of the most interesting dynamics in our economy in terms of business transformation, technological change, and new commerce. Recent college graduates have many choices in this full-employment economy, as numerous job opportunities exist and good companies are aggressively competing for the best talent. Those who come from the best schools, with the best grade-point averages, have several choices and can earn the highest compensation packages. But even if you don't fall into that category, you can still be a success by having experience, dedication, motivation, and the drive to succeed.

Twenty years ago, the young professional could join the consumer products industry, the manufacturing industry, or almost any other industry in America, and could expect within five years to move into a project management position. In ten years he or she could enter real management, and in 15 to 20 years possibly proceed on to the director or vice presidential level. Today, in the information technology industry that same career path can happen in three to five years. The pace of change in information technology is faster than in any other industry and is therefore pushing the speed of decisions, career advancement, market change, profits, and corporate growth. In keeping with this daunting pace, the expectations are tremendous, and those individuals who are willing to take on more responsibility will get the best jobs and see the fastest growth in their careers.

The biggest opportunities can now be found in the information technology industry, specifically within the Internet, networking, telecommunications, and wireless and software sectors, as these areas are demonstrating explosive corporate growth and rapid paths for career advancement. The best companies to look for are those in niches—those that are applying software or technology to new areas within Corporate America and are growing rapidly.

Some of the best early career opportunities can be found in marketing, as its importance within corporations across industries continues to develop and strengthen. Landing a job as a product manager or marketing associate, where you are involved in listening to customers, investigating and defining products, defining distribution channels, creating collaterals, and developing web-based marketing programs can only increase your own market value. Any jobs relating to the Internet are also highly sought after, whether it be a position within Corporate America, a management information system (MIS) or IT department, or with a software, networking, or Internet company. Other great positions can be found in sales training, customer service, or programming.

Information Technology Opportunities Abroad

Right now the hottest foreign IT markets for career building are South America, Europe, and Asia. Sales, marketing, product marketing, distribution marketing, and new-market penetration are essential backgrounds for these markets. In terms of potential growth, South America is in the lead, but outsourcing of information technology/services has also become incredibly popular within the European and Asian markets. Bringing new IT technology to new markets holds tremendous opportunity. The need for new technology in Europe and Asia, and the potential for market expansion, is strong.

Professionals can certainly gain experience and knowledge in these markets, especially in the newly formed Euro Market. Getting a front-line job in the Euro Market today means learning how U.S. companies can market IT products and services to a brand new marketplace—one with many intricacies and complexities, through which American companies will have to navigate in order to capture the potential profits found there. There are no experts yet in this market, hence there are tremendous career opportunities. Before Euro Market's inception, American corporations usually had several country managers who reported to a vice president of international operations. The new trend is to have two key positions, the head of international operations and the head of Euro Market, both of whom report to the CEO.

If you are interested in becoming an entrepreneur, there are always opportunities to create information technology products or services abroad at a lower cost than existing domestic ones. For example, in India, programmers will work at lower rates than U.S. programmers will. Importing IT capabilities without actually bringing in foreign labor and accompanying immigration issues will also reduce costs.

Domestic opportunities also are a great choice. Northern California's Silicon Valley, followed by Boston, have the reputation for the hottest foreign markets for IT careers across the globe. The United States possesses dynamic opportunities for action, change, and growth. Global experience can be gained by working for a U.S.-based company with global distribution channels.

New Skills for a Changing Information Technology Industry

The information technology executive needs to be netcentric in order to survive this rapidly changing industry, and this involves more than simply using your e-mail. It means being able to communicate with your web master on what effects e-commerce will have on your business. It means looking at how an extranet can provide value-added services to your customers. It means maximizing the use of your Intranet, measuring your performance electronically, and implementing aggressive technology initiatives within your own company. This netcentric concept will help you stay ahead of your competitors.

To reach this success, listen to your customers and understand their future goals for two years, five years, and so on. Your ability to anticipate the next technological logjam and transform it into profitable products and services is more critical than ever before. You need to think strategically, listen carefully, and, most important, be the first out the starting gate.

In this race for the next idea, you need to be open to opportunities that you may not have considered a few years ago. You need to forge the right strategic alliances, stay close to your competition, and take the time to know what they are doing. You also need to look at leading companies in complementary industries. What are these companies doing that your company has not yet tapped into? What knowledge do they have that you can use? How can you take what they have done and improve on it?

To be successful, you must be open to a new way of thinking; a fresh perspective; high energy, enthusiasm, and new ideas; coupled with the ability to communicate well with your customers, your peers, and your competitors. These qualities are essential in maintaining a competitive advantage. Companies can no longer rely solely on employee loyalty as a retention tool because there are fertile opportunities and incentives outside the company walls. The best CEOs know how to find and retain the best people. And the best people have the best skills.

The Internet: New Dynamics for an Exciting Career

Internet companies are a growing career choice. The Internet is hiring people faster than any other new industry in American history. What makes the Internet so dynamic, and what makes it exciting from a career perspective, is that it's moving and growing at an incredible clip and therefore has the potential to carry your career along at the same pace. The potential for growth can be found at every level, and includes rapid career advancement and high compensation rewards based on stock market evaluations and time to initial public offering. All of these items drive the intensity and excitement surrounding the Internet as a career choice.

Keep in mind, however, that a lot of new frontier exists within the information technology market. The Internet does not supply all of the answers and does not have all of the jobs. As an industry, the Internet is still sorting itself out in terms of what the key roles need to be, what the key positions are, what the right organizational structure is, and how responsibilities should be divided.

Every day there are newly created job opportunities, and these opportunities go beyond Internet companies. The use of the Internet provides huge job opportunities in Corporate America as well. Companies are moving beyond using the Internet as simply a place to promote an electronic brochure. Those companies who are able to figure out how to use the Internet to its fullest potential, including electronic commerce and building online communities, are creating new job opportunities for people in today's new Internet economy.

Big versus Small

It is important to determine what type of experience and compensation you are looking for in a position before deciding which organization will offer you the best opportunity. Different organizational sizes, cultures, and philosophies may affect your decision differently at various stages of your career.

Starting with a large corporation that is well recognized and admired by other organizations is a great learning ground. Hewlett-Packard, IBM, Intel, or Microsoft could all be classified as excellent companies in which to begin your career and gain an understanding of management processes and knowledge of company infrastructure. However, the experience of working in a young company, where you do not have access to all of the resources and support tools of a large corporation, also is invaluable. This type of environment forces you to solve problems intuitively and creatively.

As you move up through the ranks, staying in a big company as an IT executive may eventually become detrimental to your career, because there will be more qualified people vying for fewer available positions. If you are considering moving from a larger company to a faster-growth or young company, be careful to choose one that has a high likelihood of success. Obviously, there are varying levels of risk involved with young companies. If you are looking for less risk, it is probably more advantageous to choose a pre-public company that has already overcome a number of hurdles, has demonstrated a revenue-producing capability, and has developed a client base.

In the IT marketplace over the past ten years, working with the right company at the right time has created both fortunes and careers. Knowing what you know today, if you had to choose between HP and Cisco when Cisco was just starting, you would probably choose Cisco. With this young company, you could have advanced more quickly, received stock options, and had the chance to be a multimillionaire by now. It is easy to make this hypothetical decision looking back, but be sure to do your research when considering any opportunity with a young company for your future:

- Find out the strength of the board
- Determine its level of financial commitment between rounds of financing
- Check references on the founder
- Spend quality time with management team members outside of the work environment to learn what they are really like
- Do not overlook the risk you are taking

The technology may be new, the marketplace exciting, and the potential for millions of dollars just around the corner, but this is your career—so take the time to determine which opportunity matches your career goals.

Making the Switch into Technology from Other Industries

Making the switch into information technology from a nontechnology industry is very difficult. You have to be willing to take a step back in your career to gain the valuable IT experience. This may include taking pay cuts and moving down in the organization. The best way to begin the move into information technology from another industry is to become the Internet expert within your current company. Take risks, take on new initiatives and new projects, educate yourself on the latest information technology trends, and become your company's resident expert for issues relating to the application of technology. This experience will make you more transferable.

In addition, forge the right relationships outside of your company and be proactive about your career goals. This network could be crucial in a career move, as IT opportunities in another industry may not be handed to you by a recruiter because their clients often direct them to focus within comparable industries. So be creative about getting to know leaders and experts within the information technology industry by attending conferences, and by initiating dialogues and relationships by phone and e-mail. Gain rapport and relationships with targeted technology companies, and then request an interview to show them your drive and motivation.

There are Internet-based or Internet-related jobs across a wide range of industries—including consumer products, financial services, media and publishing, and entertainment. A position within one of these industries could serve as a stepping-stone into a mainstream information technology career.

Positioning Yourself for a Top Information Technology Post

If you work in the information technology industry today, you should promote yourself by delivering great results and engaging yourself with the right people. If you are not getting publicized within your current company, connect with leaders outside of your company and broaden your network. If you are not presently in the technology space, your road will be tougher, so make the right contacts, learn the technology, and make the move.

Some of the basic principles are relevant across industries, but the best way to be considered for a top information post is to deliver results and performance; develop a reputation for building, growing, and turning things around; and become known as a leader. Take the time to understand what real leadership is, and gain a reputation for results and action. Other key "positioning items" include finding mentors inside and outside of your company who are invested in your career, be willing to create your own network, and subtly promote yourself by creating your own summary about who you are and what you do.

Above all else, continue to absorb as much as you can about the industry. Know how information technology is being applied in your market or your business, know how it is expected to affect your industry, and become the resident expert.

CONSULTING

Charles W. Sweet, President,
A.T. Kearney Executive Search

CONSULTING

Charles W. Sweet, President,
A.T. Kearney Executive Search

As we approach the year 2000, we see a growing demand for management consulting services. Amid fierce competition, companies struggle to hold onto market share, growth rate, and customer base. While shareholders exert pressure for strategic growth, cost reduction, and better performance, senior executives are turning to management consulting firms for outside brainpower. These companies need to augment their internal talent with specialists in areas such as strategy, information technology, operations, procurement and supply chain management, manufacturing, and financial management.

The demand for management consulting is projected to grow 16 percent annually through the year 2000, creating a need for 250,000 new consultants in the next two years. Given the limited pool of qualified people available within the industry, and only a slim increase expected from the graduate business schools, one question echoes across the management consulting arena: Where will we get the talent? On the surface, the answer seems simple—from nontraditional sources. But upon closer examination, the answer is tremendously complex. Before dissecting this answer, however, let's look first at the nature of the management consulting business.

Industry Overview

Management consulting answers the need for innovation in many corporations. Since the downsizing of the 1980s and early 1990s, companies have focused on core competencies and turned to management consultancies to provide the functions jettisoned from flattened organizations. As the rate and pace of change increased, and the nature of change became more complex, companies found it more cost-effective to hire outside experts to create solutions to the problems of change management.

Today, consultants provide products and services that create value and help clients gain and sustain competitive advantage. There has been a shift from business process reengineering to enterprise transformation, and from providing tangible results to creating value propositions. The focus now is on improving shareholder value by increasing strategic growth and reducing costs.

There is also an emphasis on knowledge management. Companies realize the importance of their intellectual capital and seek outside help to manage this valuable asset. Management consultants guide clients to identify existing knowledge, to cultivate it, to categorize it, and to use it to generate ideas and develop new products and services.

Finally, there is a new awareness of the importance of relationships. Consulting firms today focus on people, not only within their own ranks, but also within the client organization. Communicating clearly and working together harmoniously builds relationships that result in success. Teamwork is essential in leading clients to solve an ill-defined problem and to find the answer that works in a specific situation for a unique organization. And creating this type of bond is beneficial in shrinking the time frame required to complete other engagements.

Opportunities in Management Consulting

Today there are broader opportunities in management consulting. The days of the consulting generalist have been supplanted by the era of the specialist. In our own firm, there are 15 areas of industry expertise and practice:

- Aerospace and defense
- Automotive
- Chemicals
- Communications
- Consumer industries
- Financial institutions
- Forest products

- Health care
- High-tech electronics
- Mining and metallurgy
- Oil and gas
- Pharmaceuticals
- Retail
- Transportation
- Utilities

In addition, there are 19 management consulting service areas:

- Executive search
- Corporate and business strategy
- Shareholder value
- Economics
- Organization
- Restructuring and privatization
- Globalization
- Business transformation and reengineering
- Change management
- Information technology strategies and solutions
- Product development and innovation
- Sales, marketing, and distribution
- Strategic sourcing
- Operations
- Manufacturing
- Supply chain integration
- Negotiations management
- Financial management and operations
- Human resource management

Clearly, the fastest-growing area is information technology (IT), which today commands almost half of the management consulting market. Its magnitude stems from IT's alignment with corporate goals, its importance in data management and electronic commerce, and its involvement in solving the Year 2000 problem. In the next five years, IT consulting revenues are expected to be greater than classical consulting, beginning with a 50-50 ratio in 1998 and climbing to a 60-40 ratio by 2002. Some experts believe that IT will account for 80 percent of the management consulting market in 2002.

In another area, the demand for strategy consulting is expected to outpace the growth of IT consulting. Strategy firms and strategy practices of larger management consulting firms yielded a compounded annual growth of nearly 20 percent during the past five years, and forecasters estimate greater growth rate through 2002. This is due to the abundance of mergers and acquisitions, the focus on global expansion, and the demand for better performance measurement methods.

On the industry side, financial institutions are the clear leader, with nearly one-fourth of the management consulting market. Healthcare and the converging industries of broadcasting, telecommunications, and computing together make up another quarter of the market share.

This diversity of career choices clearly entices many candidates. In fact, the popularity of careers in management consulting was featured in the March 1998 issue of *Fortune* magazine in an article that highlighted a survey that rated the "MBA Dream Companies." Of the top 10, 4 were management consulting firms, 4 were investment banking organizations, and 2 were information technology companies. The article pointed out that the allure of management consulting firms for the country's top MBA graduates was multifaceted. The attraction was based on compensation and good references for future career moves, exciting products and services, the variety of tasks and assignments, the dynamic nature and strong culture of each firm, the international opportunities, and the promise of immediate responsibility.

Consulting Characteristics and Skills

Although management consulting firms offer enticing opportunities for professionals, they are very selective in making offers of employment. Several core skills are essential for successful consulting careers. Candidates must have outstanding analytical skills and proven capabilities for innovative and creative analysis. They also must excel in communicating, not only in speaking and writing, but also in presentation skills.

Interpersonal skills also are important because of the focus on teaming. While the success of the whole depends on individual effort, the ability to build relationships within the firm and with the client is a driving force behind management consulting's growth. In our own company, 90 percent of our management consulting engagements in 1997 were for repeat clients, attesting to the success of our focus on nurturing client relationships.

The last of the core group of skills is project management. Every consultant is a practitioner who must execute each engagement well. This translates into attention to detail as well as holding on to the broader picture. It involves supervision of each step in the process, and following up with the necessary reports and communiqués.

Other key attributes of a successful management consultant are technical skills, especially in the specialty industry and services areas, and diversity of perspective and experience. There are also personal qualities that management consulting firms seek, including leadership, creativity, adaptability, entrepreneurial spirit, enthusiasm, ambition, pragmatism, integrity, humility, and humor. The best management consultants have a service attitude and acutely listen in order to understand the client's viewpoint. They are excellent facilitators and can read an audience, changing the conversation to smoothly move in a new direction. They are impressive negotiators, having outstanding persuasion techniques and excelling at conflict management. Finally, they are flexible, realizing that there is no longer a single-dimension business problem or only one solution to any given problem.

Tapping the Talent Pools

Recruiting management consulting talent is becoming more difficult than signing new clients, according to our chief executive officer's keynote address at our recent annual partners' meeting. The typical talent pools—graduate business schools and other management consulting firms—are not growing at anywhere near the rate of the consulting industry. And yet, these are the primary sources for new management consulting talent.

Recruiting from the top graduate business schools is a very important part of the responsibilities of consultants in our firm. In fact, it is a part of the individual performance review for consultants, and time for it is slotted during the strategic-planning process. Our interviewing process is intense and is designed to test the potential for success of each candidate who meets the preliminary criteria. Our MBA recruiters look for people who can solve problems, not just analyze data; who can build relationships, not just interact; and who can approach challenges from creative angles.

There is another avenue for beginning a career with a consulting firm such as A.T. Kearney, and this is to enter as a business analyst with only an undergraduate degree. This path involves working with engagement teams, providing research assistance and support services. After two to four years, these individuals are encouraged to return to school to earn an MBA degree. And then, if their performance merits rehiring, they come back to the firm as management consulting associates.

The third traditional talent pool is provided by other management consulting firms. These individuals are considered direct-entry consultants and are invited into the firm based on a proven track record that involves successful engagement work, a strong network of contacts, and the ability to initiate and nurture relationships with clients at all levels of an organization.

These talent pools remain as key sources for recruiting, but as the demand for consultants increases as the industry expands, many management consulting firms are looking for new sources for top-caliber talent. One alternative talent pool, which has provided both successes and failures, is industry. On the downside, too often, industry executives don't possess the analytical tools necessary to excel as consultants. They may have experience, intelligence, and contacts, but they are lacking in the disciplines essential for successful management consulting. On the upside, we have had positive experiences with industry executives who have left financial services, healthcare, consumer products, law, and other areas to go into consulting on their own. Sometimes they are hired by boutique consulting firms, where they gain more experience. And when they enter a major consultancy, they have a proven track record of positive consulting experiences.

The nontraditional arena, or alternative recruiting reservoir, also has provided an exciting group of consultants. These individuals with advanced degrees come from academia, business, and the nonprofit sector. They have outstanding intellectual capabilities and bring heterogeneity of thought and style to management consulting. Because they often offer different approaches to problem-solving, they are extremely valuable. We have recruited individuals with advanced degrees in economics, engineering, natural and social sciences, law, humanities, medicine, and technology. All have been distinctive individuals with outstanding analytical skills, regardless of their discipline. And many consultants in our firm with these alternative backgrounds have been prolific in producing intellectual capital, not only instrumental to their engagement work, but also important to the marketing efforts of the firm.

Recently, no fewer than six white papers, three monographs, and two articles for the firm's *Executive Agenda* periodical were developed by consultants who came from the nontraditional talent pool.

Consulting Responsibilities

In our company, we promise to help our clients define and execute a vision that will achieve measurable and meaningful results. We work with clients to help them gain the most powerful contributions from every part of their business—help them understand markets and competitors and create new and better products and services; help them develop stronger relationships with everyone their business touches; and help them reshape their economics through growth and productivity improvement.

The responsibility of the individual consultant is to contribute to improved performance within the client's organization by identifying problems and providing innovative, analytically based solutions. There are several steps in this process, and although each engagement is unique, there is one basic approach:

- Planning analysis
  —Test conventional wisdom
  —Discover counter-intuitive findings
- Data gathering
- Interviewing client representatives to gain perspective and learn how the organization and industry function
- Structuring analyses
  —Economic models
  —Logic frameworks
  —Quantitative analysis
- Communicating results
- Implementing recommendations—strategies, plans and practices

Using these processes, our management consulting firm takes our clients' organizations to a higher level of performance, not just on paper, but in practice. In every type of engagement, our consultants focus on making a deep, measurable improvement in our clients' products and services; in their customer, supplier, partner and employee relationships; and in their economics—or in all three. We are resourceful in the application of knowledge and seek to measure the achievements we have worked together with our clients to gain.

We have an uncommon dedication to explore every avenue for improvement—and look inside as well as outside the walls of client organizations to find opportunities. Our people listen actively, keenly understand a business, and share with clients our industry and business knowledge and perspectives. And when we create a team to work with a client, we form an "envelope of skills"—guided by consultants who are involved in engagement management and solution development.

The best outcomes are the product of constant client-consultant interaction. Those clients who know us well—and even those who are new to us—acknowledge our ability to work well at all levels of their organizations, from the board of directors to senior management to hourly employees. Clients value our unique capacity to get the most for and from people in an inspiring, collegial way. This is no accident: We believe in true partnerships and we consider clients to be full participants in change. By working interactively, we produce new perspectives that encourage and leverage the best ideas and experiences of both parties. And we leave an impact on our clients that outlasts even the business gains we bring.

Virtually all management consulting firms have techniques for examining and improving a client's business. Some use pure analytics. Some employ a standard, systematic approach. Others rely on sheer genius and intuition. At A.T. Kearney, we've found that if you understand the potential locked into every part of an organization, you can be more creative in transforming it—and in achieving powerful change.

The result of focusing the insight and experience of a management consulting team on a client's organization is improved shareholder value. The rewards for the individual consultant are the experience of working with a high-powered team comprising other consultants and client representatives, the success of creatively solving important business problems and—above all—the satisfaction of implementing a solution that results in long-lasting benefits for the client.

Consulting Rewards

In addition to the rewards gleaned from a successfully executed engagement, consultants also gain benefits from belonging to a blue-ribbon management consulting firm. Several of my colleagues say they thrive on the intellectual intensity and enjoy stretching themselves to achieve new insights and ideas. They say they are inspired by the creative teamwork, the professionalism of their colleagues and the client representatives, and the firm's commitment to quality.

Belonging to a world-class management consulting firm such as A.T. Kearney offers global opportunities and leading-edge resources. Our linkage with EDS provides a broad range of augmented services and unsurpassed technical expertise. The size of our organization—and of others like it—offers a variety of responsibilities and career opportunities. But most important, a career in the management consulting industry provides an ever-changing landscape where individuals can develop leadership skills, sharpen intellectual capabilities, and interact with a cadre of colleagues who thrive in an environment of challenge and change.

8

INTERNATIONAL

Roderick C. Gow, Executive Vice President,
LAI Ward Howell

INTERNATIONAL

Roderick C. Gow, Executive Vice President, LAI Ward Howell

As much as it is an overused cliché, the amalgamation of the world's myriad cultures into an interconnected, familiar, global village is becoming a reality. Nowhere is this more evident than in the world of commerce. Many U.S. companies are reporting that an increasing percentage of their sales derive from international operations. Coca-Cola, for example, sells 60 percent of its syrup and carbonated mix outside the U.S. borders. Forty-five percent of Boeing's $47 billion in 1997 sales came from overseas carriers. For companies that have long since established themselves domestically, international markets are the source of more rapid growth and higher profit margins. In 1997, McDonald's opened 1,794 restaurants abroad—compared with just 316 at home. Wal-Mart, for its part, added 289 units overseas in 1997, nearly twice the number added domestically; its international sales grew 50 percent last year.

With the success and proliferation of regional free trade agreements and a growing sense of global interdependence—the difficulties in Asia notwithstanding—barriers to international trade should continue to fall as the next millennium dawns. In a move unthinkable just a few years ago, U.S.-based financial services firms like Merrill Lynch and Fidelity Investments are rushing to set up retail brokerage networks in Japan, a market long closed to such competitors. Firms of all types, from cellular paging companies to consumer products giants, are rushing to establish beachheads everywhere from Buenos Aires to Bangkok. This phenomenon is involving small companies as well as large ones. Agency.Com, a tiny four-year-old New York-based web-advertising firm, opened its second office not in Boston or Washington, but in London.

As Federal Reserve Board Chairman Alan Greenspan put it in a 1998 speech entitled "The Triumph of American Capitalism," the economic and commercial system in which U.S. executives have been trained and work is becoming more prevalent elsewhere. Just so, the English language is proliferating and becoming more dominant abroad. CNN is available in 210 countries and territories, the Super Bowl is watched by a global audience of 800 million in 190 countries. Children in sub-Saharan Africa wear Tommy Hilfiger clothes, and teens in Israel line up to see the movie *Titanic*.

In turn, Americans are gaining greater access and familiarity with the world beyond their borders. More than 21 million U.S. citizens traveled abroad last year. Television, the Internet, and magazines daily import images of even the most seemingly exotic and distant locales into the comfortable confines of American living rooms. Such media and information serve further to demystify the experience of traveling and working abroad.

As with other major trends, the spread of American business culture and internationalism has serious implications for the individual professional's career. Increasingly, for corporations of all sizes, international experience is becoming a more densely trafficked avenue for promotion. A foreign posting is becoming a ticket that must be punched with increasing frequency for those hoping to end up in the upper echelon of management. CEOs today are eager to build up a cadre of people with experience overseas, who know there is a Naples in Italy as well as in Florida—and can function equally well in both. According to a recent survey of top executives conducted for us by Professor J. McCormick of Harvard Business School, 94 percent said the development of international executives was of vital importance to the future of their company.

Moving from Charlotte to Frankfurt, Germany, poses an entirely different set of challenges than moving to, say, Phoenix, Arizona. When going abroad, a manager must pack a different set of intellectual and commercial tools. Some can be picked up as early as childhood—or as late as middle age.

Acquiring Global Skills through Education

Increasingly, as part of the education process, business school students—be they in their twenties or forties—are focusing on international trade, international commerce, international finance, and foreign languages. Indeed, students who are currently in business school will find their MBA degrees may function as a sort of passport. MBA students signing on with established companies should expect to spend some significant amount of time abroad. Recruiters, for their part, are recognizing that international experience is increasingly important and attractive to newly minted MBAs. One of the main criteria people look for in a company, after all, is the potential for growth—nobody wants to start a career at a firm that is standing still. And, increasingly, growth is coming from far-flung global operations.

Aside from being able to understand the basics of the functioning of the world economy, the up-and-coming professional needs another set of skills to function in a global corporation. These can't necessarily be learned in the classroom, or picked up over the course of a semester. In fact, some of these skills may be unrelated to an individual's business background.

The first, of course, is language. Americans are notoriously bad about picking up foreign languages. But today, laughing about one's inability to make simple conversation in Spanish is no longer acceptable—just as a self-deprecating remark about the inability to use a computer is more troubling than amusing. More and more, those people who can function globally are going to be separated from the rest of the herd. And although English is becoming more dominant as an international business language, fluency in a foreign language inevitably eases entry and allows the professional to understand foreign cultures and customers on their own terms. Several years ago, the directive to managers and executives may have been to go out and study Japanese. Today, however, the languages that may be of most use to budding international executives are probably Spanish and the Mandarin or Cantonese dialects of Chinese.

The Importance of Developing Cultural Sensitivity

The collapse of long-standing boundaries has served to lessen the mystique of traveling and working abroad. There are now organized tours to St. Petersburg and Tibet, places once all-but-forbidden to U.S. travelers. But the ease of access doesn't completely erode the significant barriers to managing and doing business in a foreign country. Cultural mores and practices vary widely—in both interpersonal and business relationships. It isn't just a matter of knowing that you shouldn't show the bottom of your feet in the Middle East to somebody, or the proper time and manner in which to bow to your

Japanese counterpart. Rather, international managers must develop a global mindset. In doing so, U.S. executives face a particular challenge. They must overcome the perception on the part of many in the world that Americans are brash, overbearing know-it-alls who arrive with a big handshake, a slap on the back, and a willingness to dictate how things should be done.

Cultural sensitivity isn't just a matter of courtesy. It's good business. Companies that have been successful in a range of places abroad—Coca-Cola, Pepsi-Cola, and McDonald's, to name a few—start with a clear idea of what their distinctive product is and how to market it. More important, they have developed an ability to adapt their core products or services to local markets effectively. McDonald's serves beer in Germany, salmon burgers in Norway, and noodles in Japan.

People wishing to succeed in growing international organizations need to develop a similar type of flexibility and openness to other cultures. That includes, first and foremost, a willingness to live somewhere other than your home. People who are wedded to remaining in their house, in their home city, or in a particular region for the next thirty years, will find that their unwillingness to uproot themselves will increasingly hinder their ability to advance. When I was working at Barclay's Bank in London, it was undergoing reorganization. The company asked employees to assign themselves to one of two lists—those who were willing to travel, and those who were not prepared to leave Britain for work. Automatically, those who said they were prepared to travel internationally were for some reason viewed as being higher fliers and faster movers than those who said they weren't going to move.

In addition to being willing to move *physically*, managers must also develop mental flexibility. The ability to deal with ambiguity—which is cited by virtually all management gurus as indispensable to managers—is particularly applicable to international executives. This includes recognition that customs and ways of doing business are different in other places than in the United States. It is not reasonable to expect, for example, that customers and counterparts in Jakarta will respond to requests for information as rapidly and efficiently as colleagues in Houston will. This may cause particular problems because the internal officials to whom an international executive reports back home may be expecting the same sense of efficiency from their overseas employees. The strongest companies, however, have an internal culture, which holds employees to universal standards when it comes to interpersonal relationships, but have a greater sensitivity when dealing with outsiders.

Finally, people must maintain a sense of adventure—a sense of questing, searching and curiosity. Indeed, the interest in being an international player starts long before business school. Many of those who are most at ease in an international environment personally experienced adventures while traveling with their parents as children, or spent a junior year abroad while in college.

Positioning Yourself for an International Posting

Professionals who lack that foreign exposure, however, can take proactive steps to indicate an availability and capability for an international posting. Let it be known, for example, that you have acquired or are acquiring some language skills. Or that you are taking opportunities in your free time to travel abroad and learn. Another way is by demonstrating competence in dealing with specific ethnic cultures in the domestic market. Many companies in California, the Southwest, Southern Florida, or New York—be they utilities, banks, media, or consumer products firms—deal with large customer bases that are largely immigrant or non-English speaking. Working in ethnic marketing or an associated field can help demonstrate and build competencies in working with cultures other than your own.

Executives can also start training their minds to think more internationally by reading newspapers and magazines that are international—like the *Financial Times* or the *Economist*—or by watching the international news on CNN with some regularity. This not only makes people more informed, but helps them develop a mindset that views events and trends on a global, rather than a local, stage.

When considering an international posting, the professional should keep several key considerations in mind. Taking a job abroad may mean a sacrifice for the individual. But it's a two-way street. Maintaining and employing a U.S. manager overseas can, depending on the location, cost a firm from two to four times the expense of maintaining that person in the United States. So when a firm sends a manager abroad, it represents a significant investment in human capital.

Practical Implications of an International Assignment

The practice of the past, when expatriate managers were often set up in emerging markets as pashas in grand style, is no longer viable. But such expatriates should expect to at least maintain the standard of living they have in the U.S. At the very least, firms should make some concessions to cost-of-living differentials, recognizing that life is different in Milan than Milwaukee. Companies should also have a clear understanding of the impact of taxes, so they don't automatically assume that a paycheck will go as far in Zurich as it will in Cleveland. It's also reasonable to ask for a comprehensive relocation package, that will include moving expenses and reimbursements for a trip that will allow you and your spouse the opportunity to go over and check out the locale *before* moving there. According to our recent study, 72 percent of top executives surveyed said that assisting with relocation was an important strategy for motivating international executives.

Increasingly, there are family issues as well. According to the same study, of those refusing international assignments, 78 percent listed concerns about family as a reason for doing so. People considering a move should check to see if the company will help get children enrolled in an international school abroad, for example. And if your significant other has a set of skills, you want to make sure that you're going somewhere where they can be applied. The more remote and undeveloped the locale, the more difficult that is going to be. An accountant married to a marketing executive who is sent to London will have an easier time finding work there than in Shanghai.

Going abroad does not mean cutting yourself off—either from your home and life in the United States, or from your company. Hence, scheduled home visits are an essential part of the expatriate package. Executives and their families should be flown home at least once a year. Coming home isn't just a matter of catching up with friends and family, or catching up on the latest movies. Rather, it's a way of touching base personally with those to whom one reports at headquarters. Since e-mail and the telephone can only go so far in maintaining professional relationships, plugging into the mother ship on a regular basis can be a crucial means of reinforcing solid ties. Again, according to our executive survey, 50 percent of those refusing international posts cited fear of losing touch with the mainstream as a reason for refusing the assignment, and 43 percent cited a fear of no promotion on return.

It's also important that people embarking on an overseas adventure have some sort of exit strategy—a route back. If a week is a long time in politics, then two or three years is a long time in business. It takes at least a year to get one's feet wet in another culture and to feel comfortable there. But after two years, one should begin to think about another posting—either at home, or in another country. Multiple country experience is important, too. It helps provide a broader range of experience. And that can be key, because not all international postings are created equal. Executives should try to get some experience in a major money center—New York, Hong Kong, Singapore, Tokyo, London, or Sao Paolo. Those places are not only more sophisticated and appealing cities than many other foreign postings, but they allow executives to come into contact with higher level people in business and government. They also tend to present fewer difficulties in living. The experience an executive will have in Buenos Aires, Argentina will be qualitatively different from what he or she will encounter in Quito, Ecuador. Ten years in South Yemen may leave a marketing expert fluent in Arabic and endowed with a deep appreciation of that nation's culture and history—but that person might not come back with a true understanding of international markets.

That said, it *is* important to gain experience in secondary, less mature markets. Helping to open a new office in Khazakhstan will allow a human resources officer to get in on the ground floor of a rapidly growing sector of business. And since such operations tend to be smaller than those in more established outposts, they may afford the opportunity to develop more skills and take on more responsibility. Doing so also gives one the potential to get noticed.

Leaving a comfortable home for the strange and seemingly alien surroundings of a foreign posting can be a little overwhelming. Living in a place where you don't know the language, and are separated by an ocean from friends and family, can inculcate a sense of powerlessness. At root, however, a foreign posting is immensely empowering. The old view used to be that employees tapped for foreign postings should simply be satisfied with the location and package offered. But in an era when qualified people will be poached by competitors, employees may be in a better position to make demands. Today— and tomorrow—the crown jewels of any company will be the managers and executives with international experience. They need to be looked after, nurtured, developed, and polished.

Entrepreneurialism

David Beirne, General Partner, Benchmark Capital

ENTREPRENEURIALISM

David Beirne, General Partner, Benchmark Capital

Joining an entrepreneurial environment can be one of the most exciting career decisions that you can make. It can also be a daunting task, filled with pitfalls and unexpected and difficult challenges. But, if you are properly prepared and approach this new career path with the right frame of mind and diligence, the professional and financial rewards can be extraordinary.

In most instances, those professionals who choose this career move will be making the leap from a large or established corporate environment. Under this scenario, I have provided examples of two well-known executives to illustrate how and why they made the decision to make this momentous career shift.

Three Important Calls

In a speech recently delivered to the Association of Executive Search Consultants (AESC), Alex Mandl, chairman and chief executive officer of Teligent, recalled that the three most important calls he had received in his career had come from executive recruiters. The first call came in 1980. As a 35-year-old assistant treasurer at Boise Cascade Corporation, he appeared on the radar screen of a recruiter who was seeking a senior vice president and CFO for Seaboard Coast Line Industries, a large, diversified transportation company. As the successful candidate, Alex was eventually named senior vice president in charge of three operating subsidiaries, corporate development, as well as human resources and chief information officer of CSX, the result of a merger between Seaboard and Chessie Systems. In 1988 he was named chairman and CEO of CSX's subsidiary company, Sea-Land Services, the world's leading provider of ocean transport and distribution services. Under his leadership, Sea-Land nearly doubled in size.

In 1991 Alex received a second call from a recruiter. This time the opportunity was even more dazzling: AT&T, the multibillion-dollar communications giant, was looking for a new CFO. The position was significantly broad-based—the CFO's operational responsibilities alone were larger than all of Sea-Land. In addition, the position not only carried with it a seat at the corporate board table, but it was made clear that this job was the stepping-stone to the top of the company—to succeeding Robert Allen as chairman and CEO. By 1996 Alex had been promoted to president and chief operating officer of AT&T, with overall responsibility for directing the company's long-distance, wireless, and local communications services, as well as its Direct TV, credit card, and Internet businesses.

It was during his time at AT&T that Alex received his third most important call; this time, the call came from me. Unlike the other two previous calls from recruiters who were from big firms representing large clients, I was offering something very different. As a niche technology recruiter, I had been retained by the partners of a new venture-backed, local communications start-up in Virginia, called Teligent, to identify and recruit a seasoned communications executive to lead the newly formed concern.

A Drastic Career Move

Why would a highly visible professional like Alex Mandl, who at age 54 was a lifelong employee of the large corporate environment and just one step away from the top post at AT&T, consider making such a drastic career move? Oftentimes, the decision-making process is not clear-cut; it is frequently the result of a number of issues in one's personal and professional life which converge simultaneously to create such an opportunity. In Alex's case, three issues converged. Although seemingly wedded to the big corporate career path, he had always harbored ambitions for starting something small and building it from scratch. This entrepreneurial route, he thought, was also intriguing and fascinating. Although such a move was laden with risk, he had known others who had made the leap against great odds; despite being the target of doubters and naysayers, they seemed happy and energized. And Alex knew why. The very risk, the very uncertainty of the unknown was exciting to him. And for the entrepreneur—unrestricted by a cookie-cutter process controlled by large committees or boards where ideas and initiatives can drag on seemingly forever—the sky can be the limit. "You start with a clean sheet of paper," commented Alex of his move to Teligent. "And there's little to prevent you from doing something."

A second reason for Alex's decision to move to a smaller environment had to do with a changing market or, in his case, a new market with new opportunities. How many times have we heard of someone leaving that virtually "safe" environment to pursue an opportunity that is the idea of a friend or acquaintance? Is it a harebrained pursuit? Not if you do your homework. Naturally, with a high failure rate of start-up ventures, you can risk a great deal. But proper due-diligence can greatly decrease the downside. Again, in Alex's case, he did just that. Over a four-month period, he met with the owners of Teligent and got a solid feel for their commitment to the venture. He discovered that the new company was backed by seasoned equity partners with a broad expertise in the telecommunications industry. He also developed a clear understanding of what the founders were trying to bring to the table and knew where he could complement their ideas with his set of skills.

In addition, Alex analyzed the market they were entering to determine whether this new business could not only compete, but survive. Because Teligent was offering a diversified package of communications, including local exchange, long-distance, high-speed data, and Internet to small and medium-sized business customers throughout the United States, he knew that the new venture had a calculated chance for success. In his final analysis, the industry that Teligent was entering would be the most attractive spot in communications during the next 10 years.

A third reason for Alex's move to Teligent had to do with a changing internal situation at AT&T. Since 1991 Alex had held the key inside track positions for becoming its next CEO. But in 1995, Robert Allen announced that he would stay on in his current role for four more years. Suddenly, all that Alex had geared himself up for—the preparation, the momentum, and his internal psyche—had changed. It was time to consider another situation.

Taking Charge

More often than not, decisions made by others will serve as the trigger to look at something very different. This is particularly true in instances where the professional feels burned by a large company bureaucracy (either through being fired or laid off) or situations where that person is simply tired or fed up with his or her inability to effect change. Even if you have decided to leave your current company, many wonder why it is prudent to pursue a similar position with another large company where the same set of circumstances may again present themselves. This is where many professionals, who have worked for large companies for years, decide to finally take charge of their careers. Despite the potential risks, professionals in these situations feel that they have control and, more important, can make a difference through their own ideas.

As a specialist recruiter for the technology industry, I cannot advise you specifically as to where the best entrepreneurial opportunities lie in other industries. I can say, however, that if you are creative enough—meaning that you possess the ability to identify a marketable niche—opportunities can be found in almost any industry. In Alex Mandl's case, for example, the opportunity was to lead a new company in an offshoot of a mature industry: telecommunications. But spotting key opportunities in an emerging growth sector can be even more challenging, since less of an historical blueprint exists, creating greater uncertainty and greater risk. The upside, however, can be just as great too.

An industry that represents one of the best examples of recent emergence is the Internet. Less than five years ago, this was a relatively small business sector, still largely in the experimental stages. Today it has become a giant of technology; a multibillion-dollar market which has drastically swelled to create a myriad of entrepreneurial opportunities and hundreds of thousands of jobs with the now larger, established Internet companies such as Netscape, AOL, Prodigy, CompuServe, and Yahoo, as well as in burgeoning growth segments for existing technology companies such as Microsoft and Sun Microsystems. But because the Internet was a new industry five years ago, companies in this sector were faced with a real challenge in attracting top-level executives to the earliest-stage entrepreneurial opportunities. They had to turn largely to line professionals who had experience in other related industries, but who may not have had much exposure to an entrepreneurial environment.

The first real high-level executive attracted to this industry was Jim Barksdale. A former chief operating officer at Federal Express Company, Jim had been recruited to McCaw Cellular to become its CEO. The company was eventually acquired by AT&T, after which Jim ran its AT&T Wireless company. In 1994, I was called upon by the principals of another start-up technology company which was going to offer an Internet browser to the millions of PC users worldwide. Netscape was seeking an individual who had information technology or related management experience, but who could also make the transition to a start-up situation. My candidate of choice—Jim Barksdale. Getting Jim was going to be a tough sell, however. Silicon Valley had tried to attract great executives to early stage opportunities in the past, but the volatility of this marketplace made it difficult to interest them. But despite the obvious risks that Jim faced in jumping ship from a large, established corporate culture to a start-up like Netscape, I still thought that we could lure him away—particularly if we could convince him of the staggering potential financial rewards.

Why was the financial upside so predictable? The information technology industry is in the midst of the largest creation of wealth in the history of modern business. Technology and advancements in technology have given people opportunities to create billion-dollar valuations in companies within five years of inception. And that's never happened before. In comparison, it has taken companies like Coca-Cola and others decades to reach these types of valuations. However, the recent acceleration of information technology, including the Internet, has enabled companies like Netscape to attract the caliber of executive like a Jim Barksdale to join as CEO and work alongside the founding entrepreneurs. We demonstrated to Jim that Netscape could become a very global, very massive company very quickly. As a result, he would not only experience an incredible psychic reward from helping to build and change an industry, but he could create massive amounts of wealth, not just for shareholders but for himself and the management team that he would subsequently attract. Did it pay off? It did. Within just five years, Netscape has become a $500 million company.

Considering an entrepreneurial opportunity is not for everyone, but anyone who possesses the requisite drive and focus is a candidate to enter this new and exciting career path. Following are some key attributes you should possess if you are considering a move to an entrepreneurial or start-up company:

Flexibility.   Probably 99 percent of all business plans that were originally written for new companies eventually turn out to be totally different from their original intent. If you plan on joining a start-up, you must be able to change direction and turn on a dime. Willingness to accept change and implement new strategies as the company's initiatives change will be the key to your success and that of the new company. The majority of executives making the switch into this type of environment are coming from a larger corporate culture where support professionals are in abundance. However, when you join a start-up, you will have to swallow your pride very quickly; if composing your own correspondence or e-mail and making your own sandwich is beneath you, don't cross over to this side. Both Alex Mandl and Jim Barksdale were among the first employees in their new ventures; I am certain that they made the same sacrifices.

Focus.   You need to develop a clear understanding of the founders' vision for the new company. Once you have accomplished this, it is imperative that you make every effort to complement their ideas with your own set of skills. The combination of the two is essential to success, so make certain that you understand your new partners' direction and goals. New companies cannot afford a two-party system; minds have to mesh from the start.

Due diligence.   Never, ever jump into a start-up opportunity without doing your homework first. In most cases where the decision by an individual to join a start-up did not work out, it was because the new person did not have a good grasp of what he was getting into. For example, if you sense that the founders or principals of the new venture are trying to do too many things at once, and in too many areas, make certain that you get clarification as to what their goals are. Also make sure that the key structures have been or will soon be put in place. These would include a well-thought-out business plan with reasonable goals and proper allocations for funding and marketing, and an overview of the marketplace, including your competition. The best way to know that you have covered all of the bases is to seek out, in advance, trustworthy professionals who can advise you of the do's and don'ts, and where to be cautious. With their assistance, you should develop a checklist, which should state your concerns and questions to be reviewed with the new owners prior to accepting the position. Remember, look before you leap.

Commitment and Attitude

You will find most entrepreneurs deeply committed to their enterprise, and so must you be if you are going to join the team. You undoubtedly work hard now—but the commitment of time and energy that you will have to devote to your new company will be at least two-fold greater. If you are not prepared for long hours, numerous creative planning sessions, and time to implement your own ideas and vision, then this type of opportunity is not for you. The proper attitude is also key. Be prepared to take a great deal of criticism, both from your partners and new and potential clients in the marketplace. A thick skin is essential here, but remember that your critics can ultimately be your best friends. Be patient and listen carefully.

ENTERTAINMENT/MEDIA

Gary Knisely, Chief Executive Officer,
Johnson Smith & Knisely

ENTERTAINMENT/MEDIA

Gary Knisely, Chief Executive Officer,
Johnson Smith & Knisely

Entertainment and media industry employment will enter the next millennium with a bang. A booming U.S. economy, technological wizardry, and more leisure time and disposable income continue to fuel the demand for entertainment and media products—and thus for job opportunities in this rapidly changing industry. In fact, the *National Business Employment Weekly* magazine predicts a 39 percent growth in new hires over the next seven years.

And even if the U.S. economy were to go into an unexpected tailspin, the forecast for the entertainment and media market would remain bright. Time and again this industry has defied tough economic times; when other industries fell apart under the strain, the entertainment and media industry floated above the fray. Some have even labeled it recession-proof.

It may seem like everything is coming up roses for the media and entertainment industry, and maybe it is. Microsoft chief executive officer Bill Gates recently invested more than $1 billion in Comcast, the nation's fourth-largest cable operator. Network television ad revenue is predicted to grow almost 5 percent annually over the next few years. Magazine ad revenue is expected to reach $21.6 billion, up 8 percent compounded annually over the next five years. Radio revenue is up 5 percent. The Internet has already tallied $1 billion in ad revenue and a 40 percent penetration in homes throughout the United States.

The demand for senior executives in the industry is also on the rise. Across the spectrum of media companies, employers—especially those which downsized—are looking to fill senior roles with candidates from outside the company's ranks. For example, Internet companies are grabbing executives from music and publishing companies, creating senior-level openings throughout the industry that must be filled.

Specific Skills Are Vital

Before you think, however, that the industry is waiting for people with open doors and open arms, read ahead. Despite the apparent wealth of opportunities, today's job market remains fiercely competitive. Flexibility and sharply honed skills are vital for success. Today, entertainment and media companies are looking for people with very specific talents. In the past, a company recruited executives and expected them to stay five to ten years. Now, companies recruit for very specific needs that will carry them through perhaps just two years. It's a much shorter thought process, as far as the cycling of recruiting executives.

Take, for example, start-up companies. They recruit executives with start-up experience. Domestic companies expanding overseas seek executives who have already set up foreign divisions. In both cases, when the ventures are up and running, the company may then look for a marketer—while the original employee most likely moves to another start-up.

We are also witnessing a lot of what we call "out-of-the-box" recruiting. Entertainment and media companies are becoming much more receptive to looking outside their market niche for the right person. Music companies are now looking for "classical marketing skills," in positions that previously were restricted to people with music industry experience. "This is a new phenomena, one that didn't exist 10 years ago," explains Pat Mastandrea, managing director of our entertainment and media search group. "Now, 75 percent of entertainment and media firms search within the industry but outside their own specialty for the right hire," she continues. "A great deal of flexibility exists within certain segments of entertainment, between book and music, for instance."

Intra-Industry Mobility Is High

In many ways, being employed in the entertainment and media industry equates to joining one massive company. An executive may move from the Viacom "division" to the CNBC "division." People move around the industry as if it were a single company, spending just a few years in each position. Behavior once branded "disloyal" is now smart—in fact, it's the proven way to get ahead. Indeed, to industry insiders, any "loyalist" who has spent 20 years in one company and one work culture now appears to be one-dimensional, inexperienced, and unemployable. As Pat puts it, "Leveraging your career by moving around will be more lucrative financially, and it will make you a much better executive."

With this new focus on specific skill sets, employers are also becoming more receptive to executive placement from outside the entertainment and media industry altogether. Functions that are most transferable from outside this huge industry include marketing and finance. Human resource opportunities are also increasing, because the industry needs people who can understand organizations and the deployment of resources. There is also a shortage of talented financial people. Risks are higher and profit margins are lower in entertainment and media companies, signaling a need for executives with strong financial discipline.

Another group of executives who may find a home in the industry are "deal-makers." Their negotiating skills will become even more vital, because entertainment and media companies, when they aren't buying assets, are entering into joint ventures and various types of legal couplings that require a combination of legal and business expertise.

Overseas Opportunities

Globalization is playing a significant role throughout the entertainment and media industry because its products, like CNN, can be seen all over the world. From an international standpoint, entertainment and media is U.S.-centric. The hot foreign markets used to be the United Kingdom and Europe. Today, Latin America and Asia are hotbeds for entertainment and media industry growth.

The United States is the center of the worldwide media and entertainment industry, and Americans with industry experience are easily exportable. While other industries abroad may not hire someone without overseas experience, the entertainment industry is more inclined to ask "Do you know how it works in the United States, and would you like to live abroad?"

It's important, however, to point out that the international and domestic entertainment markets are not mutually interchangeable. They are very distinct entities. "Executives who accept overseas assignments in this industry may wrongly assume that international experience will make them more marketable in the United States," says Pat, who finds executives for clients in North and South America as well as Europe. "In many instances," she adds, "it makes them more marketable in the international arena, without any added value in the U.S. market. In fact, it could even make it difficult to get back in the U.S. market." Before embarking on an overseas assignment, it's best to make sure there's a way back—a contract that specifies that in a certain number of years you will be moved back to a job waiting for you in the United States.

The Internet Explosion

While these employment trends are generally pervasive throughout media and entertainment, each segment exhibits its own unique hiring characteristics. Perhaps the most dramatic hiring trends can be found in the industry's fastest growing sector: Internet services. This new-media explosion far surpasses any other media growth pattern in history. The Internet has actually changed how we think about entertainment, media, and information—and service providers have changed right along with it. Phone companies are entering the cable market; cable companies are offering phone services; and everybody is offering Internet access services. In a sense, new media, or the Internet, is simply a new technology delivery system that is going to impact all business. Already, nearly 50 percent of all U.S. companies have web sites.

New York City has been dubbed "Silicon Alley," where new-media employment will jump to 120,000 in 1998, up nearly 70 percent since 1995. This means more people are employed in new media in New York City than in any other single media category.

Who is inhabiting Silicon Alley? Online services, navigation and search sites, content web sites, online local news and information networks, online databases and directories, and interactive advertising and promotion agencies, to name a few. Early success models include Amazon.com, Microsoft Expedia, and E*Trade. Other major players are AOL and CompuServe. But the risks are high: 83 percent of Silicon Alley resident companies currently generate less than $1 million in revenue.

Talent needs are acute. Internet start-ups seek seasoned general managers. Sophisticated direct marketers and business-oriented technologists are in strong demand, along with seasoned financial executives. Those well versed in the four P's of classical marketing—pricing, promotion, product and packaging—can easily find a home on Silicon Alley.

When the Internet first exploded, people conceived of it as analogous to a print media (as opposed to visual media), so some key positions went to print executives. By now, however, it's become evident that people will not read magazines and books online—and we realize that the Internet acts and reacts more like broadcast media. In fact, executives from the broadcast industry are finding their way online. The Internet, however, is grabbing people from all facets of media and entertainment.

Two years ago, the Internet was a very wobbly industry. Today it enjoys much stronger managers and healthier financial support. The risks involved with moving into new media are a lot less than what they used to be. While individual start-ups still present risk, they may provide worthwhile opportunities to get a foot in the door. Today, a much better educated and cautious candidate pool is looking more closely at business plans and equity incentives.

In the entertainment and new media industry, potential financial gains for executives are significant, even more than in traditional media. Searches for chief executive officers in very traditional media companies would seldom, if ever, consider offering equity in an existing business, but in new media this is accepted.

Entrepreneurialism on the Satellite

Another relative newcomer to media and entertainment is the direct broadcast satellite (DBS) market. It virtually did not exist five years ago. Today's DBS employees are primarily from the cable, c-band, and consumer electronics industries, with senior executives recruited from other segments of media. There is an entrepreneurial spirit in this market segment, where adaptability is a good quality to possess, and careers can advance rapidly.

Susan Denison, a partner in our New York office, puts it best. She says: "DBS is a competitive industry that looks for people who think from the perspective of the end-user, the customer. There's a strong customer service orientation because the customer can choose among multiple distributors of DBS, or stay with cable. Someone who appreciates the value of the customer and knows how to market in a competitive environment will do very well in this market."

This is a big change. Not long ago, cable operators were hesitant to look outside the mainstream for executives. They functioned much like a utility, where the customer had very few options. But now, the cable industry has had to respond to the challenges of competition, forced on it by the introduction of DBS, as well as having to face the challenges brought on by new technologies. Both cable and DBS are therefore dynamic places to work for executives from different industries.

DBS, because it is the new guy on the block, may attract professionals who are more casual and informal than those in cable. They tend to operate on instinct and wind up as trouble-shooters. Because the industry is being built from scratch, executives from cable, telecommunications, and consumer electronic companies are sought for their industry experience. However, DBS operations must also look outside the industry because of the sheer numbers of people needed and the speed at which the business is growing. Recently, for example, executives with packaged goods marketing experience began moving into DBS. "Classical marketing training with strong focus on the four P's is valuable," says Susan, who has more than 20 years of experience in cable and DBS, as well as in live entertainment/ sports.

The U.S. cable industry, to some degree, has been a model for the overseas market, particularly in programming. Foreign cable entities are very attracted to people who have been successful in the United States and are providing many interesting opportunities for seasoned industry executives. Opportunities abound in areas such as Eastern Europe, South America, and the Middle East, where new programming channels are being launched both by cable and satellite.

Change in the Ad Agency Business

The trend toward recruiting executives for specific skills, rather than solely for their level of industry experience, is perhaps most evident in the advertising world. Ad agencies traditionally promoted from within and recruited many recent college graduates who could establish themselves and move up through the ranks. "Today, there's a significant change in hiring practices at these agencies," explains Anna Kelch, who conducts senior-level searches for media, entertainment, and communication companies from our Chicago office. "They're now drafting campaigns for use in a myriad of media, including interactive and the Internet, so they're looking to hire specialists from the outside to handle these areas specifically."

Today's large ad agencies are also looking for ways to diversify themselves. "An agency might want to create opportunities for itself in a new specialty and might seek an executive from a special, targeted agency, such as interactive," Anna says. Many advertising agencies also may wish to develop a whole new attitude among their employees. In some instances, agencies are searching out people who left advertising agencies and went to the client side. "Experience on both sides of the desk is especially valuable today," notes Anna.

The Changing Landscape of Publishing

Consumer trade magazine publishing is thriving, as is book publishing, but pressures from other media like the Internet present big challenges in these markets. The face of executive recruitment is changing. Just ask Peter Eldredge, the former *Newsweek* publisher, and now one of my partners in New York. "It used to be that smart, literary people with bachelor's degrees and master's degree were okay, but today MBA graduates are preferred," Peter says.

In book publishing, a sales and marketing background with expertise in financial management is crucial these days, in light of the rising costs of both paper and postage, and encroaching competition from online booksellers like Amazon.com. "Although it's generally an exception to hire from outside the industry, a book publisher would absolutely consider a candidate from a major book retailer to fill a senior position," adds John Malcom, another partner in New York.

Classical marketing skills become even more important in the face of increased competition from other media. You have to answer this question: What is the market saying, and how do we keep consumers interested? "Opportunities abound, in light of the recent downsizing, which depleted many publishers' bench strength," Peter advises.

In consumer publishing, it's no longer enough to simply publish a great magazine. Today, a foreign edition, trade show, cable show, and the Internet are all considered part of the package. This will create vast opportunities in the years ahead. "While the core of the wheel continues to be the magazine, there will be various spin-offs that are consistent with the editorial product," explains Peter.

Today the bulk of the publishing staff on a consumer magazine may be marketers who can package plans with the magazine's advertisers. The plans may include sponsorships, trade shows, or a web page, in addition to advertisements in the magazine. "People in these positions must be terrific marketers who can capture the essence of what the client is saying and apply it to the different media," says Peter. "A hot position in the years ahead will be a strategic marketing director of special projects who can close these two-and-three-year deals."

Live Entertainment and Sports

Another exciting form of entertainment that's now evolving and will present opportunities in the years ahead is live sports and entertainment. Traditionally, sports franchises and leagues were relatively unsophisticated mom-and-pop organizations. That's changing today as professional teams, leagues, and arenas begin to recruit high-level executives from the entertainment and media industry. There are even MBA programs that focus on live sports marketing.

At this point, however, the transition to live sports and entertainment can still be difficult for the professional manager. "While it's attractive and exciting, the sophistication doesn't match the need yet," says Susan Denison. "It's in the early evolving stages." She predicts there will be more demand for professional managers who have had true profit-and-loss responsibility. "College graduates see it as a hot, fun area," she notes.

One final thought. Fewer than one in three openings for presidents, chief executive officers, and their direct report positions in the domestic entertainment and media industry is filled through a retained search firm. That means most of the jobs will be filled by professionals who do their own homework. The entertainment and media industry is the premiere networking industry. More jobs are found through networking in this industry than anywhere else. Therefore, landing the position you want may just come down to your reputation, third-party introductions, and people you know.

HEALTH CARE

*Jordan M. Hadelman, Chairman and CEO,
Witt/Kieffer, Ford, Hadelman & Lloyd*

HEALTH CARE

Jordan M. Hadelman, Chairman and CEO, Witt/Kieffer, Ford, Hadelman & Lloyd

Dynamic, aggressive, challenging, exciting, and bold. Those words describe the *new* world of health care, an industry that until recently might have been more aptly described as a lumbering giant—large and powerful, yet awkward, slow moving and even slower to change. While the industry as a whole still has a way to go to reduce bureaucracy and fragmentation and to encourage innovation, it's quickly making up for lost time. As it approaches the year 2000, health care is changing and expanding into new areas at such a rapid pace that it's second only to the information technology industry in this key dynamic.

This rapid and relentless change has spawned a new way of thinking, which has led to the creation of completely new—or at the very least, reinvented—organizations. These include integrated delivery systems (IDS),[1] managed care organizations (MCOs),[2] and physician practice management companies (PPMC),[3] among others. To support these new concepts and organizations, new functions and positions are emerging.

Ten years ago, few would have imagined physicians voluntarily exchanging the surgical suite for the executive suite at an MCO. Or, that the technology wizard in the hospital information systems (IS) department is now seated at the senior executive table of the system's headquarters as chief information officer (CIO), advising the CEO on IS and business strategy. Organizations that have expanded their reach over several states now may have a CFO for the Eastern *region*, while a specific product or service line may require a "vice president of home health services." And I'm sure that the CEOs of MSOs[4] or medical foundations[5] did not envision those posts when they entered the marketplace a few decades ago.

A health care career offers recent graduates and middle- to senior-level executives unequalled opportunities for variety, advancement, and entrepreneurial and intrapreneurial ventures. And, while other industries may boast those same claims, only health care adds a uniquely attractive ingredient to the mix—the personal satisfaction that comes from knowing you play a role in making the world a healthier place in which to live. In an age when careers are pursued as much for individual fulfillment as for financial rewards, the need to make a difference in the world is a strong incentive. Let's investigate this industry further to see what you can expect from a management career in health care, and what it expects from you.

Launching Your Career

The dilemma facing college seniors anticipating a health care career is not unlike the one facing most soon-to-be grads—whether to pursue an advanced degree, or enter the workforce first to gain practical experience. Depending on the individual and the career that he or she is contemplating, compelling reasons can be made for pursuing either option.

In health care, there is a definitive reason for graduate school: compensation. The student with a master's degree in business administration, hospital administration, public health, or a related field can expect to earn $10,000 to 15,000 more than the individual with an undergraduate degree alone. You don't want to put yourself at a salary disadvantage at the beginning of your career and have to play catch-up throughout the rest of it.

With degrees in hand and a health care residency or fellowship under your belt, now you're ready to put that schooling to work. Here are a few guidelines to consider as you think through your options and evaluate your offers. For your first job out of college, I recommend giving the highest priority to choosing the *industry* segment and the *individuals and/or organization* you will be working with. *Location, function,* and *salary* follow, in that order.

There are many different segments to the health care industry, including: payers (insurer), providers (hospital or physician group), pharmaceutical companies, medical product manufacturers, and governmental bodies or associations. And each affords the health care professional a very different perspective and environment. After thoroughly researching these options, ideally you have narrowed your focus to one and have identified the cutting-edge organizations or individuals in your area of interest.

Your goal is to work for the industry leaders to ensure a solid foundation to your career. The work style and habits that you develop in your first job will impact subsequent opportunities. The actual position itself is less important than the reputation of the organization you work for and the executive who is committed to helping advance your career.

For your second job, however, the mix changes. While *industry* remains at the top—you want to develop a solid track record in your chosen area—*function* and *salary* take on more importance. Now that you have education and practical experience, where you have demonstrated the value you bring to an employer, you can be selective. And you need to be, because you're likely to hold the second job for a longer period of time than the first. Look for a position that offers growth, the opportunity to make significant contributions to the organization, and a salary on par with your increasing responsibilities. Acquiring knowledge and accumulating skills add to your value, which is key to keeping yourself marketable throughout your career.

New Positions

Pursuing a career as a health care executive used to be pretty clear-cut. Get a master's degree in health administration, gain practical experience during a residency at a hospital, graduate, and begin work at the hospital where you conducted your internship. Congratulations, your career was launched.

While that scenario still exists, the emergence of different types of organizations or expansions of others have created many new options to explore. CEO posts need to be filled at MCOs and PPMCs, as well as in the traditional settings, and even in hospitals there's the *hospital* CEO and the corporate *system* or IDS CEO. In addition, there are vice presidents of managed care, network development, surgical services, provider relations, and business development, to name only a few.

Several senior-level positions that are increasing in demand are: physician executives, chief information officers, compliance officers, and chief nursing officers or executives. And, making a strong comeback is the senior-level human resources executive. Here's the latest on the top posts in health care:

Physician executives.   This is an interesting phenomenon: the term physician executive was considered an oxymoron until a few years ago. Who would have thought that these professionals—clinically trained to focus on a specific area, encouraged to be decisive and to act independently—could make the change to big-picture thinking, consensus building, and becoming team players? But they have, and their clinical skills and patient focus have become essential elements in reshaping the delivery and payment of health care. To meet the demand for greater consumer and insurer accountability, these clinicians-turned-executives use their medical expertise to address the complicated issues of quality care and outcomes measurement. The titles they are frequently assuming include: chief medical officer, senior vice president of medical affairs, or medical director.

The reasons vary for why an increasing number of physicians are moving into medical management. In a 1996 Witt/Kieffer survey, 45 percent of the physician executives surveyed said that they "had a desire to be part of the health care solution," while another 36 percent said that their "interest in management/leadership challenges" led to their decision.

Can we document the growth of the profession? Yes. Since the 1980s, the American College of Physician Executives has mushroomed from a small group to its current membership of more than 13,500. Physician-specific MBA programs are also on the rise. And at Witt/Kieffer, the number of physician executive search engagements has doubled during the past year.

Chief information officer.   Finding qualified candidates to fill chief information officer (CIO) positions is about as difficult as keeping up with the frenetic information technology explosion. Every health care organization needs to manage its clinical and financial data and to integrate IS with the overall business strategy of the organization. Yet health care is competing with every other industry for highly qualified IS leaders, and unfortunately not every CIO is up to the particular challenges that health care presents.

CEOs, CIOs, and directors of IS at health systems, integrated delivery systems, and managed care organizations were surveyed by Witt/Kieffer in 1996. Nearly 70 percent of the responding CEOs said that they did *not* believe their CIOs were prepared to meet the informational challenges presented by the ongoing changes in health care. Among the numerous shortcomings that CEOs perceived in CIOs were: "a lack of strategic orientation; too much focus on process at the expense of operation goals; a lack of understanding of health care, especially of clinical operations and managed care; a lack of management and leadership skills; and a lack of 'system-wide' vision."

In fairness to CIOs, until recently there was little perceived demand for strategically-oriented IS executives in health care organizations, and few had the title, nor the direct reporting relationship to the CEO. With the growing influx of IS professionals from outside the industry, and by developing internal IS staff members who exhibit the leadership potential, a new generation of highly skilled and well-rounded CIOs will soon emerge.

Compliance officer.   Another frequently sought-after health care executive is the compliance officer (CO). Expanding from a "function" to a full-fledged "position," the CO is assigned the responsibility for steering the organization through the growing regulatory and legal maze of reimbursement, antitrust, and antifraud issues—no simple task.

Adding even more pressure to CEOs, in February 1998 the Office of the Inspector General and the Department of Health and Human Services released their final compliance program guidance for hospitals. The directive is clear: formal compliance programs should be developed by the governing board and senior management, and communicated throughout the organization.

In a Witt/Kieffer poll of 1,000 CEOs from hospitals and health systems, almost 40 percent of responding health care organizations report that they currently employ a CO or corporate compliance officer. Of the responding organizations that currently lack a CO, 44 percent say they *will* hire one within 12 months, and 29 percent say they *may* hire one within 12 months. The survey respondents identified the top three reasons for the current demand for COs as being: "[the] need to develop a corporate compliance program; [the] desire to improve the organization's ability to comply with Medicare and Medicaid billing practices; and [to] reduce the organization's exposure to civil/criminal penalties."

Regarding appropriate CO "credentials," internal audit/public accounting and law tied at 39 percent each as the ideal professional backgrounds for COs, according to the CEOs surveyed. An additional

15 percent of CEOs mentioned financial management as the ideal background.

Chief nurse executive.   Talk about an evolving profession! After years of struggling to gain the respect of physicians and administrators, many nurses are now joining their colleagues in the executive suite and making decisions that directly impact patients and the future of the organization. Whether the title is chief nurse executive, chief nurse officer, or senior nurse executive, make no mistake, the position is up at the top. Nurses are making the move from providing hands-on bedside care in a single department to designing a comprehensive strategy for quality of care for all patients in the system.

Nurses' clinical expertise and patient-focused approach to care serve them well for the role of chief nurse executive, but other skills also must be present to complete the executive profile: strategic thinking, a vision of integrated health care delivery, business development acumen, management experience, good physician relations, political savvy, and financial skills.

For the nurse who is interested in moving up the administrative ranks, a 1996 survey of CEOs and senior nurse executives conducted by Witt/Kieffer and the American Organization of Nurse Executives provides some suggestions. When the CEOs were asked to address "the single best way for nurse executives to advance their careers in today's healthcare arena," they offered the following blunt advice:

- Lose the nurse mentality—think globally.
- Move away from task-oriented clinical areas and into finance and marketing.
- Seek responsibility for leading and managing initiatives that result in major change for the organization.
- Be a visible representative both inside and outside the organization.
- Broaden experience and education beyond traditional nursing areas.

Although the door to the executive suite is now open to nurses, they still face a few hurdles—mainly the mind-set of some of their colleagues. On the upside, however, some CNEs are not only feeling at home in the executive suite but have begun to sit comfortably in the CEO chair, too. Still others have used their hospital expertise to launch independent health care businesses. Either way, a nursing career affords many options beyond the traditional roles once so closely identified with the profession.

Human resources (HR) vice president.   Highly skilled, senior-level HR executives are in demand and hard to find. Like so many other health care positions, the role of the human resources executive has grown in complexity along with the organization it serves. While the staples of recruitment, retention, benefits, and compensation remain in the HR Division, even these basics have taken on new proportions or structures through mergers, acquisitions, or the emergence of such entities as PPMCs. Some of the additional functions that the senior-level HR exec is expected to perform are:

- Negotiating labor contracts
- Understanding regulatory changes
- Preparing environmental analyses
- Melding employee benefits from two merged organizations
- Creating a unified organization or corporate culture when the entities may be scattered across one or more states
- Implementing continuous quality improvement or total quality management programs throughout the organization(s)

In June 1997, Witt/Kieffer polled members of the American Society for Healthcare Human Resources Administration (ASHHRA) and asked them what traits and skills were most critical to their career success. These results were compared to a similar survey of hospital and health system CEOs and found to be in sync. Both ASHHRA members and the CEOs identified strategic thinking, vision, and being values-driven as the most important attributes an HR executive can possess. Both groups believe that HR executives should focus on planning for the future of their organization, whatever its type. At the same time, however, HR vice presidents realize they must relate well to specific audiences such as other senior executives, board members, physicians, and employees.

Astute HR execs are looking at the big picture—they're broadening their skills and increasing their scope of responsibility as it pertains to refining *any* operating system that involves people. And that's good, because it's what their CEOs expect and need from this key player on the leadership team.

New Skills

A changing industry naturally requires its leaders to continually update and add new skills to their portfolios. "Good communications skills, ability to lead, ability to build coalitions, skilled at physician relations and good management ability" ranked as the top five desirable traits of CEOs in a 1997 Witt/Kieffer survey of IDS CEOs.

Another skill to add to the mix is obvious: computer fluency. Savvy communicators who have Internet addresses and linkages are using them to reach out into their local communities—and to participate in online symposiums across the Atlantic. Physicians practicing in rural clinics can tap into the research capabilities of the academic medical center in another part of the state or the world. Information, like knowledge, is power, and you need to know how to access it immediately with a touch on the keyboard.

And of course you need to have an open and curious mind, especially about subjects and industries outside of your current profession. Interest in executives from outside of health care is increasing. In many cases, as CEOs take the helm of an IDS or MSO, they are creating organizations that did not previously exist. As a result, governing boards and search committees are looking for CEOs outside of the traditional health care models. Non-health care executives interested in making a career change could find a home in the health care industry—particularly from the banking and airline industries, because they offer a new perspective to historically ingrained problems.

In fact, a health care background or an accounting degree won't necessarily move you into the chief financial officer (CFO) post of a health care organization any more, but experience outside of the industry could. Witt/Kieffer recently filled a healthcare CFO post at Emory University, Atlanta, with an individual who had been a partner in a Big-Six accounting firm, the treasurer and CFO of a large U.S. city, and most recently, the CFO of the Atlanta Committee for the Olympic Games. The firm also placed the former treasurer of Delta Airlines into the CFO position of the international help organization CARE-USA. These are just two examples of what may become a trend in health care hiring. The message here is clear: broaden your experience or associations outside of the traditional domain.

Job Search/Switch

As with any other profession, there are certain fundamentals that apply to job-seeking or career transitioning: networking and attending health care meetings. You may be tired of hearing this, but networking with individuals who are in the field you're interested in is invaluable. If you are a student, talk with your professors, the parents of your classmates, and neighbors for contacts in your areas of interest. If you're a professional with marketplace experience, call your colleagues, alumni office, neighbors, club members, civic or social contacts, and so forth. Student and professional alike can attend conferences conducted by national professional organizations, and then join or get involved in their activities. Their publications and conferences provide the proverbial wealth of timely information on trends and issues of concern to the group. Many also offer career tracks or sessions at their programs and job referral services, and all provide ample opportunities to meet people in the careers you're exploring.

Many outstanding professional societies for health care professionals exist. Here's a partial listing:

- American Association of Health Plans, Washington, DC
- American College of Healthcare Executives, Chicago
- American College of Physician Executives, Tampa
- American Organization of Nurse Executives, Chicago
- American Society for Healthcare Human Resources Administration, Chicago
- Healthcare Financial Management Association, Westchester, IL
- Healthcare Information and Management Systems Society, Chicago
- Medical Group Management Association, Englewood, CO
- National Association of Health Services Executives, Silver Spring, MD (represents African-American health care executives)
- National Managed Health Care Congress, Atlanta

Even though I've laid out a specific path for the young health care executive, let's be realistic. The days of one career in a lifetime are long gone—four or five are more likely. And, as I mentioned previously, non–health care experience is currently an asset in health care, since many CEOs are designing organizations that have yet to exist. In fact, your health care career may not yet be on the radar screen. Expect to blaze a trail unique to your interests and experience, whether you're a recent graduate or an experienced manager.

Positioning

What does it take to get to the top in the health care profession and stay there? According to system CEOs surveyed by Witt/Kieffer, the following traits are critical for career success now and will be during the next five years:

vision, strategic thinking, personal integrity, the ability to adjust to change, and the courage to be a risk-taker.

Whether you are a recent college graduate or a seasoned pro, my advice doesn't waiver on the basics of career building. In addition to the previously noted leadership traits, consider the following:

- *Develop your skills.*   Consider yourself in your own personal CQI or TQM program. Always be on the lookout for opportunities to learn more about technology and marketing, along with being on top of industry trends.
- *Increase your visibility internally and externally.*   Volunteer for committees or task forces in your organization. This gives you exposure to colleagues in areas outside your immediate department or division. The same is true for your involvement in a trade or professional society, civic or community group. This experience enables you to make business friendships outside of your organization, thereby exposing you to a wide range of opportunities.
- *Seek more responsibility.*   Take on additional assignments or the tasks no one wants to do in your organization. Be known as a "can-do" or "whatever it takes" kind of employee, who doesn't just meet expectations but surpasses them.
- *Find a mentor.*   There's nothing like developing a good relationship with a well-positioned business colleague who is on the fast-track and willing to take you with him or her to the top. Forty-two percent of the respondents in our previously cited Physician Executives' Survey reported having had a mentor who played a pivotal role in their careers. And the physician execs who reported having had a mentor were more likely to be promoted, earned higher than average salaries, and had vice-president or higher titles.
- *Be a mentor.*   In the search to find a mentor, don't overlook the advantages and opportunities to being a role model to your colleagues or those who report to you. More than 60 percent of the physician executives who reported having a mentor are also mentoring others. Regardless of what position you hold, do your best and be willing to offer your support and guidance to those around you.

Before I close this chapter, let me expand on one of the success traits identified in the survey: integrity. The dictionary's definition of integrity is "honesty, sincerity, uprightness." It almost sounds "quaint," doesn't it? Yet it's one of the "must-have" characteristics listed by our clients when they're describing the next leader of their organization. Live your values. Maintain your integrity.

Now is a great time to enter the health care industry. You may very well have a part to play in reshaping the delivery of health care for future generations. Opportunities are plentiful and will continue to expand for bright, aggressive, innovative, and energetic individuals who thrive in a stimulating, fast-paced, and ever-changing environment.

Whether the position calls for systems integration, new-business development, or improved methods of patient care, the overarching goal in health care is the same regardless of the organization, and it's a noble one at that: offering the best services and/or products possible, at an affordable cost, to assist individuals in enjoying healthy lives.

Endnotes

1. Integrated Delivery System (IDS): an organization that is composed of other organizations that offer various components of healthcare services, with the goal of increasing efficiency and profitability. For example, an IDS may include one or more hospitals, a medical group practice, clinics and perhaps, a health plan and/or long-term care facility.

2. Managed Care Organization (MCO): "an organization that assumes the combined responsibility and risk of financing and delivering care at a predetermined level or reimbursement." A *Guide to Recruiting, Hiring and Training Managed Care Executives*.

3. Physician Practice Management Company (PPMC): a legal entity that provides administrative and management services to physicians, owned by investors.

4. Management Services Organization (MSO): a legal entity that provides practice management services to a hospital, physician or physician hospital organizations.

5. Medical Foundation: "an independent organization of physicians, generally sponsored by a state or local medical association or society, concerned with the delivery of medical services at reasonable cost. Some foundations are organized only for peer review purposes or other specific functions." Joint Commission *Lexicon* of health care terms.

PLOTTING THE COURSE

BIG CORPORATION VERSUS SMALL COMPANY

*Paul R. Ray, Jr., President and CEO,
Ray & Berndtson*

BIG CORPORATION VERSUS SMALL COMPANY

Paul R. Ray, Jr., President and CEO,
Ray & Berndtson

It's the age-old question: "Does size matter?" There was a time when debating the benefits of working for a big corporation versus those of a small company led to an easy answer for that question: "Of course, size matters." When you entered the workforce, the first place you looked for a job was with the big corporations. You learned your way through the business trenches, you earned your stripes, and you moved up. Most professionals expected to spend their entire careers with those companies, while some left to work in the more entrepreneurial world of small business.

Today, largely because of reengineering and downsizing, the playing field for that decision process has been leveled, making small companies a much more viable consideration throughout one's career. Today's implied contract between employee and employer says that "as long as I'm getting the opportunities to develop in my career, and as long as my company is pleased with my performance, I will continue to work here." Clearly, this contract does not discriminate between large and small companies.

In addition, unlike 10 to 15 years ago, it is no longer a detriment to your career to move back and forth between small and large companies—as long as you can demonstrate positive development as a result. In fact, more and more frequently we are seeing companies that consider it an asset for a professional to have gained experience in multiple companies of different sizes. The once-distinct differences between working for small and large companies have begun to melt away.

Against this backdrop of changing attitudes, the question of whether to work for a large or a small company has become less a decision about the companies and more a decision about you and your current needs. These needs should be based on your preferred work style, your goals for development, where you are on your path through life, and finally, where you stand in the course of your career. The important thing to consider is what kinds of experiences you want and need to round out your career and your life.

Large versus Small—An Overview

A big company offers the growing professional more infrastructure—more training, more support, and possibly more resources to help him or her gain experience in a particular function or business area. With this infrastructure comes the opportunity to focus on a specific area until you fully understand it and can add value to it. In a large company, you will likely have more people with whom you can share experiences and from whom you can learn. This support system can serve as an incubator for new ideas and approaches. In a big company, you'll learn how to perform your function well and, by working with others, see how your area fits with others in the company.

In a smaller company, you'll probably have to gain experience by doing— jumping into a project and learning hands-on. It's also likely that you'll be given a wider realm of responsibility through involvement in several aspects of a project rather than just one. You may have to make more independent decisions more quickly—which can be both exciting and risky. There will likely be fewer people to learn from and bounce ideas off of. In a smaller company, you will be learning and doing at the same time, and your work— good or bad—may have a bigger and more noticeable impact.

How Big Is Big?

Or better put, how small is small? For the advertising executive in a regional agency of 50 people, moving to a new job in a national agency of 400 workers may feel like a long leap from small to large. On the other hand, for the regional sales manager of an international computer company with more than 100,000 employees, accepting a position as vice president of sales and marketing for a software developer with 1,500 people will be quite a culture shift in reverse.

The Small Business Administration (SBA) defines a "small business" as one with fewer than 500 employees. Amazingly, more than 90 percent of all companies in the United States fall into this category. But however you define a small company—as self-employed, 1 to 19 employees, fewer than 100, or fewer than 500—the U.S. economy is still dominated by the giant corporations that compose that other 10 percent of businesses.

Addressing Your Wants and Needs

There are no one-size-fits-all definitions of what a megacorporation can provide you compared to its more diminutive counterpart. It would be inaccurate and unfair to make a blanket statement that says only large companies will offer you long-term security and better benefits, and only small companies will offer you a job you'll love and a higher quality of life. However, with that said, there are some generalities that should be understood when considering your current wants and needs and what role the Davids and Goliaths of the business world will play in addressing them.

Your Career Path

Like everything else, a full career has a distinct life cycle, with a beginning, a middle, and an end. Your current location in that cycle should be considered when looking at a new job in a large or small company:

- If this is your first job or if you are currently out of work, restricting your job search by the company size could make the search longer at a time when you can least afford to wait. Assuming you aren't living off of lottery winnings, it may be unwise to reject any offer that promises good opportunity, regardless of the size of the company. Even so, it is still important to understand what you can expect from a large versus a small company. You will be better prepared to ask questions and negotiate your offer. In addition, you won't run into any unexpected surprises when you begin your new job.
- If you have been in the workforce for a number of years, you may be considering your next career move. Have you spent the majority of your career to date in small companies, developing a broad range of expertise? Or have you been in a large corporation, refining your skills

in one general area of expertise? Maybe now would be the time to consider moving from one type of company to the other. A career with a variety of experiences will be more valuable and, in the long run, more fulfilling.

- Perhaps you are in the final years of your formal professional life. With careful planning and a little luck, you've had a successful and fruitful career made up of many rewarding experiences. You're not ready to formally retire, but you would like to shift gears. In all probability, this is not the time to consider a move to a large corporation, except at the most senior levels. You have years of valuable experience that many small companies would find extremely beneficial.

Your Work Style

In today's jargon, this is often referred to as *cultural fit*. In other words, it describes how well your preferred work style fits with the way your organization conducts business. Are you more productive when left by yourself to work through a task independently? Or do you function better as part of a team that builds on its members' combined ideas? Are you more comfortable in a company with a flexible structure, where your responsibilities may vary from time to time? Or do you prefer an organization with a well-formed hierarchy and clearly defined responsibilities?

These are examples of criteria that could define a company's culture and the questions you might ask yourself to assess your own fit with that company. In many ways, small and large companies have their own distinct cultural characteristics:

- Employees in small companies may work together more as peers than as bosses and employees. Small companies offer a more entrepreneurial feel in which people often work on interdisciplinary teams that combine sales, marketing, production, accounting, and so on. In fact, you may be expected to have working knowledge—if not actual skills—in areas outside your realm of expertise. In large companies there may be entire departments for each discipline of the company, and you may seldom deal with anyone from outside of your specialty. Many large companies, however, are finally beginning to recognize the value small companies provide their employees and have begun to structure themselves along more interdisciplinary matrix lines.

- Historically, large companies have been able to offer executives more support. This meant that professionals had a well-defined realm of responsibility and knew who was available to help them fulfill their projects. In small companies, executives often wear more than one hat, which means the tasks they work on tomorrow could be an about-face from what they are doing today. In many ways, this distinction is becoming less clear as large companies continue to downsize and begin to outsource many of their support activities to smaller companies.

- Based on the "big fish in a small pond" theory, the opportunity for recognition of a job well done is higher in a small company. In large companies, more people may work on one project, and individual efforts may be lost in the shuffle. However, the best of the large companies develop management with an eye for detecting talent and good work and recognizing it appropriately. That recognition just may take a little longer.

Development Goals

Throughout your career, you should periodically take stock of where you stand and where you want to go. When you know your destination, you can determine what you need in order to get there. Is it specialized training? More experience? A different kind of experience? Whatever it is, small and large companies can each give you something different:

- Small companies offer a variety of work on a number of projects. This often includes the opportunity to manage a project from A to Z. This type of experience can be especially valuable for sampling different ways of working. The value is getting immediate experience in the real world. The danger is becoming a jack of all trades but master of none. While breadth of experience is important, depth of knowledge in your specialty area is essential—especially during the early and middle stages of your career. In large companies the work you do may be similar from day-to-day and for some become repetitive. On the other hand, practice makes perfect, and if you want to develop true depth of knowledge in one area of specialty, that may be the way to do it.

- The start-up time, or period before which managers expect significant contributions, may be longer in a large company. In other words, if you need time to develop skills to fill your role, you might have it in a large company. Small companies may expect you to hit the ground running. When they hire someone, it's usually to fill an immediate need, and low overhead prevents them from supporting you for an extended period of time. Often, small companies can't afford to give new employees long start-up periods.

- During your tenure at a large company, you may have multiple occasions to attend special training courses or seminars. These companies have the time and resources available to provide these opportunities. While small companies recognize the importance of developing their employees, outside training and development may be more of an indulgence. The best small companies though, are creative about building their own development programs by making use of the knowledge available from coworkers, vendors and clients.

Stage of Life

Accepting a new job is an important turning point in one's life. Whether a job is right for you should be heavily dependent on what other milestones you have reached on your path through life. Are you a recent college graduate considering your first steps into the business world? Are you a newlywed with aspirations of buying your first home? Has your family recently grown with the addition of a new child? Are you about to send your first son or daughter to college? Is it time to begin considering how you will spend your retirement years?

These and other issues will determine whether you have the luxury to take a job that has some element of risk—or one that provides more stability. These considerations may help you decide whether you can afford to exchange comfort and security for doing something with more risk. The characteristics of small and large companies weigh in heavily when addressing these questions:

- In the past, large companies were considered to provide more job security than small ones. While large companies may be able to provide a longer learning curve, assurances of long-term employment are not as definite today as they were in the days of our parents and grandparents. It's not unusual today to pick up the newspaper and read about more layoffs in a Fortune 500 company. (What you may not read about, however, is how often these same companies are able to rehire or move those laid-off employees to different parts of the company.) A small company with a proven track record can often offer as much or more job security than a large one that may have grown out of control. Small start-up companies, on the other hand, have the highest level of risk and the highest rate of failure. The best examples in this area are start-ups in the technology industry. Of course, getting in on the ground floor of a small new company can be exciting and in the long-term very rewarding. If you're willing to accept the risks that come with these volatile ventures, the payoff can be tremendous.

- In large companies, it may be easier to address major changes in your way of life. Suppose your spouse accepts a job in a different city, or you decide to make a change in your career path. For employees who have demonstrated their value, large companies often have the ability to address these issues through adjustments involving geographic relocation or transfers to different divisions within the company. To move up or make dramatic life changes in the world of small business, you may have to actually change companies.

- A big company offers more opportunity for lateral moves to new areas of focus. Just a few years ago, lateral moves were considered a weakness. People were expected to move up the ladder in the chosen area. Now, with flatter organizations even in big companies, lateral moves provide a way to develop new expertise without changing companies. A lateral move today, say from finance to operations, generally enhances your career rather than detracting from it. In smaller companies, exposure to a breadth of experiences and areas is more likely to happen automatically—but if it doesn't, this deficiency is difficult to overcome without changing employers.

Finding the Job

Job opportunities in small companies may be more difficult to uncover, because small companies often don't have the resources for nationwide or even regional advertising or to retain the services of a professional recruiter. As a result, they may limit marketing their open positions to local newspapers and personal contacts. However, with the phenomenal growth of the Internet, many small companies have begun tapping this resource for publicizing their positions nationwide at minimal cost.

It also stands to reason that small companies will have fewer jobs available. A small company may need ten sales people, while a truly large company may require a sales force of thousands. Simple logic tells us that at any given time, the large company is more likely to have an opening in its sales department than the small company.

Whatever the size of the company, the first step is learning as much as you can about it. With the explosion of information available on the Internet, there is no excuse for approaching a company uninformed. The Small Business Administration (*www.sbaonline.sba.gov*) is an excellent resource for information about small businesses, and each year *Fortune* magazine (*www.pathfinder.com/fortune*) publishes a list of the best large companies to work for in America. If you don't have access to the Internet, your local public library is an excellent resource for researching companies.

Once you've identified the company and the position, the person you want to see is the one who makes the hiring decision. With fewer layers of management to go through, gaining access to that individual is usually much easier in a small company than it will be in a large one. In addition, the decision-making process will most likely be much faster in a small company, because there are fewer people involved in the process. In a large company, getting hired may be a much more formal and bureaucratic process.

Making the Move—Large to Small or Small to Large

In today's environment, there is no longer a stigma associated with switching jobs or moving from a large company to a small one. In fact, in many cases, the broader range of experience you can demonstrate the better. Whichever situation you are considering—large to small or small to large—play to your strengths.

Small companies appreciate the cachet that a well-recognized corporate name lends to their management teams. At the same time, you should be prepared to demonstrate that you have the flexibility to work in a company that may have less structure, less support, and require a more hands-on approach than you're accustomed to. For many, this change and the opportunity to make a significant impact quickly are the very things that attract executives from larger companies.

When moving from a small to a large company, you have the unique advantage of experience in a variety of disciplines. Tailor your resume and interview responses to highlight the experience that is most relevant to the position in question. Emphasize your ability to think outside the box.

Does Size Matter?

Remember this: The days of lifelong employment with a single company are gone. While in many ways that fact benefits the employer, it can also be good for you. If you decide that the company you are working for doesn't offer you everything you need, learn what you can, do your best work while you're there, and then move on without hesitation or regret. Regardless of size, there's no company from which you can't learn something—even if it's what *not* to do next time.

So . . . does size matter? Absolutely. But not in the same way it used to. Today, knowledge matters more. The keys are solid experience in your area of specialty and a broad understanding of how what you do fits into the company as a whole. By carefully planning your career to include a variety of experiences, you will be able to demonstrate that knowledge to any company—large or small.

A TICKET TO THE TOP: WHAT FUNCTIONS ARE THE POWER BASES TO SENIOR-LEVEL MANAGEMENT?

Windle B. Priem, Vice Chairman and Chief Operating Officer, Korn/Ferry International

A Ticket to the Top: What Functions Are the Power Bases to Senior-Level Management?

Windle B. Priem, Vice Chairman and Chief Operating Officer, Korn/Ferry International

I recently read that to protect its computer system, a single Fortune 500 company has budgeted more than $600 million to combat the "Year 2000 Bug"—the electronic megaglitch resulting from the faulty assumption that 23:59, 12-31-99 marks the end of the world. This news was a reminder of how dramatically the business world is changing as we edge toward the new century. Companies are now devoting resources to challenges that didn't exist as recently as 10 years ago.

The good news is that so many organizations are beginning to make regular and substantial investments in the future. And the future, after all, is where all of us will be stuck before very long. Corporate executives are giving thought to a wide range of issues that were not even on the radar screen when I began my career as an executive search professional 22 years ago.

Today, most executives instantly see the wisdom of ensuring that their companies' electronic systems stay up and running. They readily accept the need to search imperfect computer programs for errors. But are they equally committed to debugging their own careers? How many are searching their own minds for flawed assumptions that can skew their professional trajectories?

It happens all the time. Vast numbers of eager young executives rise from entry-level jobs or emerge from MBA programs. They enter the ranks of corporate decision-makers; then, within a decade, the careers of many stall, and they may even drop out altogether. Some find success in other occupations that suit them better. But many once-promising careers are derailed by poor, unexamined assumptions.

Some of these assumptions are repeated so frequently that they appear to be self-evident truths. And it is easy to see how they take hold: in many cases, they represent the prevailing wisdom lined up on the business shelves of airport bookstores. They are repeated endlessly in glossy magazines and on the luncheon circuit. But are they true? Are they useful? Will they lead to sound career decisions? This chapter presents a gadfly's view of the most pernicious, career-threatening bugs.

The Millennium Bug

The first is the executive version of the dreaded "Year 2000 Bug": the premise that entirely new rules will guide corporate life in the new era, that there is a fundamental disconnect between past and future. Too many executives have bought into the wrongheaded notion that the personal and professional qualities that led to success in the twentieth century will have little relevance in the twenty-first century.

Just think of all the business books that have touted the new millennium as a brave new corporate world, calling for new kinds of organizations and new kinds of executives to run them. All of those publications are right—and wrong. To be sure, they have shed light on key trends—the impact of the information explosion; the growing importance of a company's human capital; the promise of emerging markets. But in profiling the successful executive of the twenty-first century, they have seriously underestimated the importance and appeal of enduring leadership qualities.

Executive recruiters hear all the time about the new and different nature of leadership in the new millennium. In my view, this talk is 50 percent useful and 50 percent hype. And it is sometimes difficult to know which is which. In the search business, we are uniquely positioned to measure the gap between what corporate decision makers may say when they speak to the Rotary Club or contribute an article to an in-flight magazine, and what they actually do when it comes time to choose new leaders for their organization. They may describe a next-generation executive, reengineered for the new century. But more often than not, they are drawn to the candidate who has the same mix of qualities that has always added up to success in business. They want someone who is willing to work unbelievably hard, make personal sacrifices, communicate a powerful sense of mission, and stay focused on the issues and challenges that will determine the organization's long-term success.

Corporate America's heavy hitters all have these qualities. General Electric's Jack Welch is a case in point. Welch is widely admired by his peers; J. Tracy O'Rourke, CEO of Varian Associates and former chairman of the National Association of Manufacturers, has called Welch "without doubt the most outstanding CEO in the world right now." To be sure, Welch is an innovative leader. His emphasis on the human dimension, and specifically on employees' continuous learning, reflects the vital role of knowledge management in today's business environment. But the qualities that earn him his high praise would set him apart in any era. As O'Rourke puts it, Welch just keeps "doing very well—over and over and over—no matter what the world economy is doing."

The New-Age Bug

A close relative of the Millennium Bug, the New-Age Bug is an attractive and therefore dangerous specimen. It infects executives' career programming with bromides that sound so familiar that they are accepted without question. These notions have the personal appeal of the human potential movement, and they often contain a grain of truth. But in the competitive context of the corporate world, they often turn out to be fundamentally unsound. And they often sound harmless, but I have seen them undermine some very promising careers. Here are a few examples:

> *Work smarter, not harder.*   No one would argue against working smart—
> maximizing efficiency and boosting productivity. But I'm skeptical
> when I see "career management tips" in magazines or on the Internet
> that counsel executives not to work too hard. This piece of advice,
> downloaded from a site called CareerLab, is typical: "Extreme work
> enthusiasts—workaholics—overproduce and overachieve, but then
> burn out, and some never recover. If you're working 80 hours a week,
> every week, something may be wrong. The Golden Mean, 'Modera-
> tion in all things,' is not a bad idea." Sounds reasonable. But I have
> spent decades observing and analyzing why companies hire and hold
> on to some executives and send others packing. And I've never seen a

candidate's name cut from a short list because he or she works too hard. I've never seen a corporate leader lose the confidence of the board for getting to the office too early or for staying too late.

A good family man—or woman—makes a great corporate leader.   Because strenuous work and long hours are viewed as signs of commitment to the organization, balancing work and family is hard and getting harder all the time. Successful executives take a strategic approach to this challenge, as they do to all of the problems they encounter. But they do not permit themselves the illusion that their company's board or shareholders are eager for them to spend more time with their families. Some companies are instituting more family-friendly policies, but the hard truth is, most individuals who land top corporate jobs show the willingness and capacity to make significant personal sacrifices. They are, above all, available—to work extended hours, absent themselves from home, make long trips on short notice. This is one reason that the glass ceiling has been so difficult for women to shatter. To their credit, many extremely able women have been unwilling to put aside family responsibilities for long stretches of time. In my experience, family-friendliness is making a limited impact on corporate culture, but it does not yet influence the outcome of high-level searches. There is a direct correlation between executives' willingness to make personal sacrifices and their ability to nab the highest-paying jobs.

Job satisfaction is more important than job compensation.   I often hear this from highly motivated candidates, who want me to understand that the chance to take on a compelling challenge or oversee a brilliant team is worth a great deal. But in my experience, in business the best jobs also pay the most. Moreover, companies are more willing than ever before to reward strong leadership. In recent years, average CEO compensation has risen much faster than corporate profits. The same web site that warned against becoming an "extreme work enthusiast" got it right in summing up compensation: "People tend to earn what they deserve to earn."

The Backwater Bug

Of all the buzzwords of the nineties, "global" may be the most pervasive. The business media have produced countless features about the global executive, global marketing, and global perspectives on a wide range of corporate issues. Many of these features bewail the parochialism of American executives, who speak foreign languages poorly if at all and can use cross-border postings to hone their cultural and negotiating skills. The assumption that global is good is so ubiquitous that it has crept unseen into executives' consciousness. And to be sure global is good—sometimes.

But when companies decide who to hire and how much to pay, global experience is apt to be less important than other factors. I often find it instructive to study companies' explanations of their hiring and compensation strategies. The *Wall Street Journal* recently ran an article about the decision, by the board of a major bank, to increase substantially the compensation of its chief executive. Four key reasons were cited: his success in boosting the bank's profitability; his progress in creating a singular franchise position, in effect branding the bank; his prowess in managing the human dimension—getting the right people in the right positions; and his sustained emphasis on quality. Expertise and experience in managing a global enterprise were not mentioned.

To be sure, some foreign postings pay off in the long run; but do not count on an overseas assignment to jump-start a sluggish career. It is important to stay in a place where your contribution is visible—and most of the time that still means a job that keeps you walking in and out of the front door of corporate headquarters. Moreover, in today's volatile world, a posting that promises to make your career one year may break it the next. Some of yesterday's plum assignments—including jobs in volatile Asian markets—are looking a lot less attractive today. From the standpoint of my search clients, years spent in a backwater business setting do not confer the status of "global executive." They may not weaken your candidacy for top jobs, but they do not automatically open doors. Debugging your career means thinking realistically about where you want to be and why.

The Zigzag Bug

The corporate ladder has given way to a more complex, multidimensional structure, with multiple routes to the top. Nontraditional career paths have become the rule, not the exception. This is the common wisdom, and it leads many executives to the conclusion that they can zigzag their way to the top. But like most common wisdom, it is true . . . and untrue.

It is true that in a lineup of usual suspects, the "alternative" candidate commands attention. But while he does stand out, he seldom gets the job. Our clients often say, at the outset of a high-level search, that they would welcome a nontraditional candidate. They seem to yearn for new vision. They acknowledge the organization's need for fresh thinking. But most of the time, they end up selecting an outstanding individual from within the same industry—a "known quantity" who has established a strong reputation and solid track record in a similar setting.

There are exceptions, of course. Numerous leaders with remarkable talent and drive have survived the leap from one industry to another. Louis Gerstner of IBM is a case in point. One can also find examples of executives who have moved successfully from one culture to another, like Jean-Pierre Rosso of Case Corporation and Mano Kampouris of American Standard. Large corporations, whose chief executives must be able to thrive in the glare of the media, are sometimes more willing than smaller companies to reach outside their industry or borders for an especially charismatic leader.

Corporate decision-makers may say, with all sincerity, that they want to move "out of the box," that they are willing to make an unusual choice. But for the most part, they do not walk the talk. When the time comes to name a new chief executive, convention tends to hold sway. This is understandable. Everyone involved with the search knows that the stakes are extremely high, and the impact of the decision may be immediate and dramatic. Stakeholders in the company, especially institutional investors, will not be shy about exercising their influence and protecting their interests.

It is not stodginess that causes corporate boards to avoid an unorthodox or surprising choice. When companies venture from convention, Wall Street can serve as a very effective reality check. The value of a company's stock has been known to rise or fall significantly—by 5 percent or more—based on shareholders' reaction to a newly named chief executive.

In spite of all of these reasons, choosing a nontraditional career path can still lead to the executive suite, but it involves significant risk. As you make career moves, you need to take a realistic look at the course you are charting. If you are eager to move to a different industry, change your direction sooner rather than later, so that you will have time to establish a track record that will attract the notice of corporate leaders (and their search consultants). Don't lurch haphazardly from one job or industry to another, but do make strategic moves reasonably often. Our clients tend to resist candidates with experience in only one company, especially if that company is not moving forward.

Career strategists plan not only moves from one industry or company to another, but also moves from one function to another. The strongest candidates for top corporate positions tend to have experience in both staff positions (having headed up finance, marketing, or human resources, for example) and line positions (having run a division and been accountable for the bottom line). Today, a handful of top executives are emerging from functions once considered dead-ends. One case in point: David D'Allesandro rose from corporate communications to become president of insurance giant John Hancock—the youngest senior officer in the company's history. This is not altogether surprising. In today's flatter organizations, chief executives deal more directly with employees, and powerful communications skills are more vital. Moreover, today's CEOs are under intense pressure from corporate directors to manage and protect the company's public image (and their reputations).

The Lightning Bug

The lightning bug corrupts executives' thinking with the faulty assumption that innovation, especially in the realm of technology, is the key to success and must be pursued at all costs. They make heroic efforts to stay current with emerging trends and master next-generation systems—demonstrating flashes of brilliance as they dart from one new development to the next. But in the process, they may lose track of enduring values. They may neglect critical competencies. Most importantly, they may lose focus.

The lightning bug tends to afflict executives who take too literally the admonition oft repeated by best-selling business gurus: *The only thing you can count on in today's business world is change itself.* It turns out that in the corporate setting, there are a number of other things that matter. Leadership tops my list. By leadership I mean the capacity to motivate and inspire people, to drive them to excellence and unleash their creativity. I mean the ability to formulate and communicate a vision of the future.

In short, leadership involves defining reality, not only for employees, but also for investors, customers, and suppliers. Felipe Cortes, president of Mexico's Hyslamex, puts it this way: "My role is to give my team a point of view. As leader, I must analyze and give my team constant feedback on market trends; competitors; emerging opportunities; government and investor relations; market threats; and issues related to our parent company. . . ." In an era of information overload, this requires the ability to sift, from a constant, overwhelming influx of data, the knowledge and trends that truly count.

There is no question about it—technology plays a crucial role in business today. Successful leaders tap the power of new technologies. They ensure that their organizations can respond quickly and nimbly to changing conditions. Effective oversight of an organization's knowledge base is more important than ever before. But at the end of the day, interpersonal skills often carry more weight than technical prowess. Managing information resources inevitably involves managing human resources. In the future, there will be a much higher premium on the executive who is a very skilled human resource manager.

In truly great companies, the chief executive assumes personal responsibility for key human resource decisions. This is something I have observed over and over again, especially in the financial services sector. There is a direct correlation between a company's healthy growth and the chief executive's personal commitment to sound investments in its human capital. The most successful companies are those where CEOs spend a third to one-half of their time ensuring that they have the right people in the right positions. Jack Welch does this at General Electric. So does Ned Johnson at Fidelity, and Frank Cahouet at Mellon Bank. They have seen the light. Twenty years ago, most chief executives were more than willing to delegate all personnel matters, including selection of key managers. Today, they ignore these decisions at their own peril.

The Synergy Bug

Synergy is a New-Age expression of the age-old principle that in business, the whole is more than the sum of its parts. Cooperative interaction among a corporation's parts—whether teams, divisions, or subsidiaries—can indeed create an enhanced combined effect. When groups of people pull together to accomplish a common objective, the results can be truly dramatic. That is why many search professionals are now asked to consider not just individual searches, but an organization's larger human resource picture. Moreover, in today's flatter companies, where information circulates freely among coworkers, collaboration is more frequent and more important than ever before.

But in their efforts to advance their careers, some executives have relied too heavily on their credentials as solid team members. When Sony chairman Norio Ohga was asked recently which characteristics will lead to success in the future, he answered succinctly: an entrepreneurial spirit. Tomorrow's executives will not seek mere jobs; they will look for opportunities to apply their knowledge and skills to new challenges. They will be able to function in many kinds of organizational settings, including both team and individualistic environments. And they will be prepared to work for themselves as independent contractors.

To compete effectively, today's executive needs to come to terms with a paradox of the modern corporation: Collaboration is essential to a successful organization, but individual initiative remains a key to a successful career. There are times when being a loyal team player can stall a career. You have to want to be a winner. And you have to be able to spot other winners a level or two above you. Wrangling an assignment with one of them is a good way to position yourself for advancement.

Getting a Firm Grip on Reality

All of the aforementioned bugs, undetected, can derail your career. Now is the time to get rid of them. The bottom line: To succeed in today's business world you need, above all, a firm grip on reality. You need to look beyond the best-sellers and the buzzwords. Be prepared to challenge the gospel. Take a good, hard look at all the sacred cows. Powerful organizations do this: They are willing to throw out even the most appealing or deeply entrenched policies and procedures if they don't work. The same principle holds for individuals. You need to look critically at your own assumptions about the business world and your place in it. And you have to be prepared to discard those premises and practices that are unlikely to get you where you want to go. That is what I mean by debugging your career.

Suggested Reading

Almstead, A. "CEOs Promoted from Without: Companies Seek Fresh Blood, Proven Track Record." *ABCNEWS.com*, March 9, 1998.

The Economist Group and Korn/Ferry International. *Developing Leadership for the 21st Century*. 1996.

Hesselbein, F. "Journey to Transformation." *Leader to Leader*, no. 7, winter 1998.

Kuratko, D.F., and Hodgetts, R.M. *Entrepreneurship: A Contemporary Approach* (3rd ed.) Orlando: Dryden, 1955.

Miller, William H. "Leadership's Common Denominator: Here are Thoughts from Some of the World's Top CEOs on What it Takes to Lead Effectively." *Industry Week*, August 18, 1997.

The Minority Candidate: Charting the Course for Men and Women of Color

Herbert C. Smith, Chairman, H C Smith Ltd.

THE MINORITY CANDIDATE: CHARTING THE COURSE FOR MEN AND WOMEN OF COLOR

Herbert C. Smith, Chairman, H C Smith Ltd.

Most minority candidates in today's workforce know about the events of the 1960s, when there was a major effort to ensure equality in hiring and promotions in organizations. The process of achieving equal employment opportunities for minorities actually began more than 20 years earlier, however, when in 1941 President Franklin D. Roosevelt issued an order to defense contractors to cease discriminatory practices in hiring. This initiative encouraged broad-based employment and at the same time launched a human resources strategy that continues to this day. All over America the human resources issues associated with public and private initiatives have focused on bringing minorities into the mainstream of businesses and organizations. Leaders from minority group categories can now be found in responsible positions in business, education, and government throughout the country. Although it has taken more than 50 years to reach this point, the evidence indicates that these leaders are making increasingly substantial contributions to organizational growth. And these individuals are inspiring and encouraging others to persevere and to follow similar career paths.

Nevertheless, as we approach the new millennium, diversity in the workplace continues to be an emotional hot button that elicits both positive and negative responses from people at all levels, and in all industries. Everybody has an opinion on the subject. And, however we describe the national strategy to give people from all backgrounds a foothold in organizations, the ideal of total equality still remains elusive, and the means of attaining it is still controversial.

Although well-educated, talented men and women from minority groups have realized substantial gains from a broad range of programs designed to attract, develop, promote, and retain them, the reality is that many are still at risk. New opponents of workforce management methodologies are emerging in the courtrooms and in the court of public opinion. Affirmative action, sexual discrimination or harassment, and lifestyle decisions have become code words for the new hot buttons as we move into the next century. Middle to senior level minority executives have to achieve maximum performance in an environment of turbulence, change, resentment, jealously, and envy. Moreover, against the backdrop of major structural adjustments in business, education, and government, organizations have outsourced and reengineered—resulting in fewer levels of management. "Careerism" has given way to "employability." Minority professionals are competing for fewer and fewer leadership roles. There are tough questions being asked regarding their future in all types of organizations.

Individuals seeking to join corporate organizations would do well to learn about the minority pioneers who have retired. Ask corporate recruiters about the level and type of positions held by minorities, their length of service, and the career tracks that these men and women of color pursued. If middle to senior level management is the career objective, minority candidates need to become more proactive as mentors, coaches, and sponsors of people like them. Remember that each generation in a corporation must raise the bar and set examples for others. It is expected (but not often stated) that men and women of color must be better than their counterparts.

It could be said that the presence of highly qualified middle to senior level minority professionals in the private arena is the direct result of a series of government initiatives. Corporations doing business with the government are required to meet different standards of contract performance. As a result their workforce represents a broader fabric of society. It is clearly evident that more than ever our elected and appointed officials in federal, state, and local agencies reflect the diversity of the communities they represent and serve. Public and private companies have followed this lead, though at a much slower pace. In the private sector, many organizations are conducting advertising and marketing campaigns designed to recruit and promote a more diverse workforce. These organizations cite business reasons as the chief objective. Another factor in this trend is that the characteristics and level of human sensitivity of the current crop of chief executive officers in companies large and small are very similar to those of the emerging group of minority and women professionals seeking middle to senior level positions. The major challenge for these organizations remains the development and retention of this talented workforce.

The goal is to field the best team of players in order to remain competitive and profitable. Using a sports analogy here is appropriate. During 1998, President Clinton convened town meetings on the subject of race in America. One such meeting took place on April 14, 1998, and focused on the sports industry. In some ways, sports typifies the ultimate setting for people of different backgrounds working together as a team to achieve the ultimate goal of winning. This is certainly what we see as we watch sporting events. Sports also provides the one audience that crosses all racial and social lines. Behind the scenes, in the executive, coaching, and ownership ranks, the sports industry struggles with the same issues of workforce diversity as other major industries. But the hurdles are slowly being crossed, and teams are getting the message. Professionals who are seeking these career opportunities will become free agents with their services going to the highest bidder.

Development and Retention

With a cadre of minority men and women in leadership roles firmly established in organizations, a constant issue in their development and retention is mentoring. Everyone, regardless of race or gender, who makes it to the middle-to-senior management level has a mentor. This was true in the past and will continue to be so into the next millennium. It is what the "old boy network" and the "new people network" are really all about. It is generally accepted that these executives gained positions of increased responsibility because the concept of managed careers was a part of the rules under which people entered the workplace. This continues to be the case. Human resources departments are struggling with how to foster informal mentoring that keeps talented individuals, regardless of race or gender, in organizations while preparing them for increasingly responsible challenges.

A self-development strategy linked to future business plans should be an evolving process for everyone. For men and women of color it is an absolute requirement for survival and growth. We recently recruited a candidate

with a distinguished military career and outstanding educational achievements. A Fortune 500 company selected this respected African American.
In order to make the transition from the military to corporate leadership he
was hired into a position where his strengths could be used immediately.
Concurrently, he requested that he be sponsored for courses at the Harvard
Business School to learn more about strategic planning methodologies. He
continues to work and attend courses to further his career. Leading author-
ities of self-directed learning and career development support this idea and
link professional growth and development to three factors. These include
(1) individual initiative, (2) demands of the job, and (3) the organizational
environment in which the business operates. Self-directed learning and
continuing education are valuable adjuncts to job performance. Other pro-
ponents see the need for a self-development strategy as a requirement for
understanding that careers as we have always known them will not exist in
the next decade.

Long tenure in a company with a succession of positions is fast being
replaced by a series of applied experiences. Successful completion of these
activities with measurable results tied to concrete accomplishments leads to
a set of competencies that allow individuals to adapt to a variety of roles and
responsible positions. An example is a candidate hired from a major consulting firm. For a year and a half he worked on a series of merger and acquisi-
tion projects. Recently, he was appointed general manager and president of
a new venture with global operations. Self-development is a requirement for
everyone in organizations because new skills are mandatory. No longer will
individuals spend 20 to 30 years in one company doing one job. It is a new
day. Those who grow and are retained will be generalists.

Successful individuals now climbing the corporate ladder will become
mentors and models. Make contact with them. Write or call for an appointment to visit at their office. Obtain interviews, build relationships, try to
understand what they do, how they persisted, and what lessons can be
learned from their experiences. Follow up with a thank-you note. The message is to take charge of your career, establish a legacy characterized by flexibility and creativity, and help others along the way. The issue is how to get
and keep current and grow professionally. Perhaps for the first time in more
than fifty years, minority and majority candidates face the same hurdles,
obstacles, and roadblocks to career enhancement. Many believe that career
development is different for men and women of color. This is not the case:

Everyone is expected to produce results, to possess general management qualities, and to be prepared to compete for future opportunities.

Transitions

Despite the efforts of organizations to develop and retain key human resources, each year thousands of men and women of color consider making a change in their career paths. Many have advanced degrees, fine experiences in several organizations, and proven administrative and management skills, as well as the desire to undertake another challenge. Those considering a change should endeavor to find out how their experiences parallel other opportunities, and how they can act on this information. As with any strategy, career transition planning depends on possessing accurate information about the steps to be taken and what skills and abilities are needed, as well as being up-to-date regarding personal situations and the opportunities that are available.

A good first step is to get an understanding of the fundamentals of effective career transition planning. Using a legal pad, draw a timeline of your life from birth to age 80. Use a scale of two inches to one year. If you are 35 years old, measure 70 inches from date of birth to identify the present. Now locate and mark the events in your background that are pertinent to a new professional opportunity. List such things as educational achievements, each promotion or new assignment, presentations at conferences, commendations, and so forth. Then enter calendar milestones up to the present. Be sure to indicate the projected dates of potential changes. On the timeline mark the date "Career Transition Target."

Talk with your family, superiors, peers, and subordinates. These people will listen and give effective feedback from differing perspectives. They can offer other perspectives and perceptions about the new directions being considered. Study the qualities of successful managers and executives in organizations. This will become the focus of the new position exploration. Once this process of self-development has been started, remember to accept responsibility for evaluating your progress on a monthly or quarterly basis. A transition strategy can be exciting and rewarding. Start the process at least six months before a projected change. Be sure to keep an up-to-date listing of performance evaluations and appraisals that can be incorporated into the self-development process. Remember, you are the product. You are reinventing yourself.

Skillful Management of Career Change

Middle to senior level minority men and women executives have used appraisals and evaluations to guide the future of their associates. These provide one of the keys to maintaining a satisfactory level of employee performance. Of all the things that comprise an overall perspective of the worth of an executive, the performance appraisal may be one of the most critical measures. Similarly, when considering a career change, your own evaluations can be valuable planning tools. Review the past three or four annual performance evaluations. Current and future professional contributions are at the heart of the information the process reveals. Once reviewed and analyzed, set the course for a new organizational relationship. Build on your strengths. Your experience and the evaluations should tell you what you are good at and what you enjoy doing. The decision to defect causes individuals to spend more time on managing the career change process than anything else.

There are a few basic principles to consider. Do your homework. Find out as much as you can about a potential employer as possible. Annual reports, company descriptions, brochures, investment information, and press coverage can give you valuable insight. Talk with several people who know the company and the job opening. Look at three to five very different types of positions before deciding to join an organization. Seek situations where performance of people is the key ingredient in the selection. Minority and women professionals should insist that initial assignments have clear expectations and that help will be available, if needed. Think through the variety of assignments. Job descriptions may last a long time, but assignments change all the time and can be negotiated. Know your personal strengths and weaknesses, but focus on strengths and have a clear understanding of effectiveness and proven ability. This is a strategy that has worked very well for majority candidates. It serves no less as a model for men and women of color.

Once you have negotiated your new position, the most important step in making a change is to fully understand the position and design plans for review each quarter for a period of two years. Establish goals and measurable results. The single largest source of failure is the inability to think through and help others think through what a new position requires. Making the right career transition decision is the ultimate way of remaining current in the profession and being successful.

Knowing When to Leave

The decision to leave an organization is a crucial turning point affecting minority men and women and the company. In spite of your best efforts, your job performance can suffer during this time. The natural tendency is to think about the new challenges ahead with great enthusiasm, while performing with less vigor the old tasks that remain to be completed. Stay focused and finish your assignments completely, with the same dedication and professionalism that has characterized your tenure. You will want your former managers, colleagues, and mentors to remember your contributions to the organization. These are business relationships that continue to need nurturing and development. Returning to the company at some future time is always an option. Do not burn your bridges.

We recently recruited a minority candidate who had left a major computer company five years previously to gain experience in manufacturing leadership. A high potential performer with 12 years of service, he had left because there was no opening in his unit, and he felt he could not grow. He joined a smaller company, where he was given responsibility for manufacturing and engineering. He was recruited back to a very senior role in his former company, given a long-term contract, and has been promoted twice during the past year. He was welcomed back because he had maintained relationships with a number of key executives.

Networking in Professional and Community Organizations

Sustained involvement in professional and community organizations is mandatory for continued growth and development. There is much value in networking with other colleagues and associates. For minority and women executives with 15-plus years of work experience, the idea of networking and keeping a resume current should be uppermost on the agenda. When developing your transition plan, increase your activity in professional groups or community organizations related to a specific business discipline. Seek out opportunities to make presentations, serve on committees, conduct research on industry topics, and become more visible. In essence, do things that characterize the behavior of a developing executive. Most companies actively encourage and support participation in such activities.

Every business discipline from accounting to warehousing has a professional group or organization devoted to maintaining and improving its members. Join as many in your field as possible to get a broad and diverse perspective. Use the complex web of social relationships available through networks and professional organizations to get in front of peers, colleagues, and associates. All of these contacts can be useful and supportive in the next move. These networks can help minority and women executives explore transition issues and focus on opportunities in the marketplace. Utilize proven management skills to "get in touch" with individuals in comparable situations. Networking in professional organizations can cut through the formal process of seeking a new position. Carefully cultivated, these external groups can provide intelligence that will assist in career decision making. The National Black MBA Association has an active chapter in Europe comprised of managers and executives working on foreign assignments. Most of the members will return to the United States with greatly expanded duties and be positioned for additional responsibility. If you are not a member of the NBMBAA, now is a good time to join.

Relationship building is the key to being successful in businesses and organizations of all sizes. As minority and women managers and executives become more sophisticated in analyzing their networking capabilities within professional groups, they can determine whether there is a good fit and whether they are in sync with personal goals. When the two are at odds, minority and women managers can broaden or reshape the networks as needed. Most successful minority and women executives invest considerable time and resources in restructuring their careers. It makes sense to rely on informal and established professional groups to reestablish a broad base of social links.

Best Industries and Opportunities for the Future

Making a recommendation on where to work and what to do in the new millennium is like playing poker. One has to play the hand that is dealt. In a full-employment economy, education and a variety of experiences drawing on marketable competencies separate the winners from the losers. Men and women of color projected as leaders of tomorrow will face radically different, decentralized organizations. These managers must possess a management style which emphasizes negotiation rather than ruling by authority. Everyone will continue to experience explosive reductions in their ranks. This continued downsizing will not be confined to large organizations. Small to medium-sized companies will also reduce management faster than ever. The same can be expected in the military and in government.

One way to compensate for the loss of positions is to make the roles more expansive, more demanding, and more challenging. Flattening the organization and rotating middle- to senior-level minority men and women executives to more and different assignments will be commonplace. Organizational boundaries will disappear and the span of control will get larger. Technology will permit individuals to provide leadership over large groups of people. These skills are in more demand, and break from the hierarchical organizations of the recent past.

Industries of the future that offer significant areas of growth include forest products, distribution and logistics, financial services (new banking, insurance, and investment services), health services, technology and research-based companies, and manufacturing of all kinds. There is also a mushrooming of entrepreneurial organizations fueled by the constant downsizing of middle to senior minority men and women management talent. Hospitality services such as cruise ships and resorts are serving an ever-growing group of Americans and foreign constituents, and offer a full array of positions and opportunities. Perhaps the most explosive growth will occur in the communications and entertainment industries, where a combination of business organizations will come under single ownership. One thing is certain, almost every week there is a shakeout in business. Mergers, acquisitions, alliances, and partnerships split up companies and change the lives of people.

Ticket to the Top

Minority men and women can position themselves to move to the top of the corporate ladder. Do what the organization demands and requires. Above all, be patient. Only in America are younger people in key leadership roles. Rapid change in the structure of organizations brings the elevation of the mature leader with good judgment and a proven record of steady growth and profits. Moving from managing to leading is not an easy step. Management is an art, and leading is a science. Leaders set the tone and provide the vision and drive for the organization. Leaders often march to a different drummer. Rarely do they represent a style for all times and for all people.

They possess traits that many minorities in executive positions have demonstrated.

Leaders foster maximum effectiveness through common performance measures with partners inside and outside of the organization. Leaders have good ears and open-door policies associated with access and channeling for mutual achievement of goals. Most leaders constantly define, shape, and use core values to rediscover and review the things that make the organization function better. Leaders are experts in a specific area, while embracing those concerned and involved with the organization. They understand the use of relationship power in dealing with others. The key to being a leader for the future is determined by the way the executives embrace all aspects of leadership.

Men and women of color selected as leaders possess strong egos, the ability to think strategically, are oriented toward change, and believe in the fundamental value of human behavior. They are politically astute and have strong convictions. They know how to use power and how to be flexible and effective in making decisions. Leaders of the future will have to pay attention to social issues more than ever before. The environment and a just society will demand more attention of the next generation chief executive officer than did previous generations.

The Global Perspective

The landscape has changed forever with customers, competitors, and opportunities going global. It is like the American gold rush. Even small entrepreneurial companies are expanding in ways that were not possible just a few years ago. It is estimated that more than 300,000 U.S. citizens are on assignment throughout the world, and this does not include military personnel. The largest and most respected business organizations show a solid trend toward more global placement of executives. Global operations are the result of international mergers, start-ups, acquisitions, and joint ventures. Men and women of color should actively lobby for postings in the global arena.

Be prepared to move immediately. During a recent round of business golf, a middle-level sales and marketing manager was called and given two weeks to move to Brazil to head up a three-year project on cost reduction in procurement. We continue to communicate daily via electronic mail systems. Global assignments have become the most fertile ground for development into key leadership roles.

Minority men and women executives aspiring to change careers will find it advantageous to look outside of the United States. New and exciting opportunities exist. Global assignments are becoming the choice for executives who want challenging destinations and diverse experiences. Different cultures call for different behaviors. Physical demands provide exciting challenges. We cover 4 time zones in the United States; however, around the world there are 24 zones. Global executives are the newest ambassadors for America. Going global is the next business frontier. It is where tomorrow's decisions are being shaped today. And more and more of the executive decision-makers on that frontier will be men and women of color.

RETURNING AS THE
EXPATRIATE EXECUTIVE

Dwight E. Foster, Chairman, Foster Partners

15

RETURNING AS THE EXPATRIATE EXECUTIVE

Dwight E. Foster, Chairman, Foster Partners

The global enterprise has been well established within the lexicon of today's business terminology. The multinational corporation (MNC) dominates world business. Multinationals exist in several varieties:

- The large institutionalized model, such as General Motors Corporation, IBM, UniLever, and PepsiCo
- Rapid-growth, instant MNC technology-based companies, such as Microsoft, Oracle, Sun Micro-Systems, and Intel
- Slower-growth manufacturers of machinery and equipment, seeking to ensure their planned share of global business
- The domestic company with dreams of becoming a global player

All of these initiatives are fueled by executive leadership at the managing director and senior management group level. The MNC has an appointment business risk. Can these executives perform successfully at the country level? The executive has a career risk. What is his or her fate if the overseas business unit performs below expectations in the eyes of the corporate parent?

International appointments are announced with corporate bugles blowing and flags waving as departures are made to overseas postings. Reassurances are made relative to times of stay and career paths back to the home country. Group executives and human resources professionals are sympathetic and sincere during the bon voyage phase of the executive's transfer. But once landed, the executive must face up to the realities of his or her posting. The focus of this article is on the plight of the U.S. international executive seeking to return when things go wrong in the overseas posting. The plight, however, is a global one. It has been the writer's experience that German, French, Japanese, and British expatriate executives go through similar career issues. The return jobs they are offered as reentry points often represent reductions in responsibility in contrast to the management latitude they held in the United States.

The expatriate manager in many countries operates in a community of expatriate managers. This is particularly true in non-English-language countries. His or her primary contacts are within their industry segment or with expatriate managers in their communities, along with occasional contact with folks from headquarters. During his or her assignment abroad, the expatriate manager may receive unsettling danger signals:

- The headquarters company may be under-performing.
- International operations are being reorganized from geographical to worldwide product-line management.

Or finally,

- The executive who approved the manager's transfer, the company's top international executive, has either resigned or been fired. (It's difficult to differentiate between resignations and firings these days.) The result is that a great many expatriate managers have suddenly lost their sponsor.

Let's try a case study. We'll call our subject Charley Jones. Our Charley Jones represents a composite profile of a great many international executives Foster Partners has observed over the years.

Charley Jones is 38 years old, an MBA graduate from a top business school, who is provided the opportunity to transfer to the European headquarters in Brussels. Charley's company, High-Liver Corporation, is a packaged goods company holding dismal number 3 or 4 market share positions in most major Western European markets. High-Liver is very excited over the prospect of taking a leadership position in the newly opened Eastern-bloc countries.

Charley Jones joined High-Liver following a graduate school internship. He spent his early years in a succession of headquarters and financial analysis jobs and observed that the division presidents had all come up through marketing. Charley obtained a transfer to a business unit as an associate product manager, and his career took off in a succession of promotions.

Charley Jones gains his first look at international operations during one of High-Liver's frequent task force studies. He makes an impression on Ralph Black, the president of High-Liver's international division. Sam Smith, Black's human resources vice president, invites Charley out for a long lunch. Sam points out the need for Charley to gain line international experience. High-Liver's leaders of the twenty-first century must have international experience. Without it, managers like Charley are unlikely to be considered for upcoming senior leadership positions available in the year 2000.

Charley bites and accepts a transfer as director of marketing for Europe, reporting to a French multinational managing director, who is within three years of retirement. It is hinted that Charley could be a successor candidate for the incumbent managing director. Charley transfers with his wife, Beth, and children ages 7 and 9, anticipating that they will enjoy a posting of three years' duration that could lead to six should he be selected as the next managing director for Europe. Then it would be back to the United States, where he is certain to be a candidate to succeed Ralph Black. Charley sees an inside track straight to the top of High-Liver.

The European subsidiary turns out to be a shambles. Marcel Frontenac, the managing director, believes that Charley has been forced on him as a spy from headquarters and undermines him at every step. Marcel, while very good at lunch, is rigid, below plan, and resistant to change. He is surrounded by long-term cronies and blames the subsidiary's under-performance on the poor and stale U.S. products adapted for the European market. Marcel assigns Charley to study an aggressive market entry into Poland and Russia.

Charley tries to see Ralph Black on his next visit to the United States. Black's secretary says that he is unavailable, but suggests that Charley might meet with Sam Smith. Charley bares his soul to Sam Smith. "Don't worry, Charley," Smith reassures him, "Corrective steps are being taken."

Marcel is suddenly retired two months later. His successor, Kurt Richthoven, is hired from outside the company. He has been a country managing director for Germany. Their first meeting is disconcerting for Charley. "You really haven't accomplished much this year, Charley," Richthoven comments in his perfect English. Richthoven promptly cleans house and hires several direct reports from his former company. Ralph Black and Sam Smith visit and endorse Richthoven's plan for reorganization. The headquarters is to be moved to Dusseldorf, and Charley's new job is entitled Director of Business Development, Eastern Europe. He requests a meeting with Black and Smith to discuss his future. Black cancels at the last minute. Meeting with Smith, Charley suggests a transfer back to the United States. "But you just got here" Smith reminds him. "Give it a year under Richthoven," Smith counsels. "I'm not going to mention this to Ralph, Charley. He'll get the impression that you're a quitter. Ralph has plans for you, Charley. But you have to show him what you're made of."

Let's pause now to review Charley's career path with High-Liver. A year earlier he had been a rising marketing star in a U.S. division. He had not thoroughly researched the European organizational issues, nor had he spent enough time one-on-one with Marcel Frontenac. He has had only cursory communication with Ralph Black, his ultimate leader, with primary communications passing through Sam Smith, who appears to listen well but commits little. High-Liver had provided Charley Jones with a good career prior to his overseas transfer. Should he abandon High-Liver now? Beth isn't happy about the move to Dusseldorf from Brussels. It will upset her routine. Charley agrees to commute from Brussels to Dusseldorf.

Charley and his family take a three-week holiday to the United States that summer, and Charley makes an informal visit to every major division of High-Liver. Charley's cover story is that he wants to share his Eastern-European-bloc experience with other divisions of the company. The reality is that Charley is building informal tie lines for a possible U.S. return. Charley researches executive search firms with apparent relationships with major packaged goods firms. He excludes all search firms that may have relationships with High-Liver. Charley tries to personally meet as may of the search firms as he can during his U.S. visit. Lastly, he tracks former High-Liver marketing colleagues who are now employed with other packaged goods companies. Charley's career repositioning strategy is fully underway. He begins to receive calls, but they are relative to other international marketing positions. He takes some interviews and receives one offer, which he declines as a lateral. Meanwhile, Charley makes his peace with Richthoven. They begin to work well together. Charley tells Beth they will spend one more year before entertaining returning home.

High-Liver reorganizes the following year. Ralph Black resigns and is succeeded by an outside hire, Alan Sharp, a senior managing director from the Utah Consulting Group, a prominent management-consulting firm. Sharp has been consulting with High-Liver for the last year and has been hired to install a worldwide product line system. Richthoven resigns on the basis of strategic incompatibility with the reorganization.

Charley is invited back to the United States to meet with Alan Sharp and Sam Smith. To Charley's surprise, Sharp is three years younger than Charley, and has spent his entire career with the Utah Consulting Group. "Alan could be the next president of High-Liver," Sam Smith counsels.

Sharp explains his concept of worldwide product management. The product line managers will be appointed vice presidents and be accountable for profitability. The country managers will be responsible for implementation of the product line strategy. Charley is offered the managing-director-level country manager position in France. He will report to a vice president of international operations, a fiftyish long-term High-Liver international manager named Nigel Beaumont. Nigel will operate from London following his transfer from Hong Kong. Sam Smith explains privately that Charley's career path would lie either with a worldwide product line management position or as Nigel's backup as vice president for operations. Charley is to receive a substantial pay raise and move to Paris, but High-Liver requires a three-year commitment on Charley's part. It has gotten back to Smith that Charley had been looking around. Sharp needs loyalty from his managers.

Charley, at this juncture, is ready to settle in the Paris headquarters office as managing director for France as part of the newly focused High-Liver international management team. He has general management profit and loss experience for the first time. He is disillusioned after his second operating quarter. The strategic marketing powers belong with the worldwide product line managers. As a country managing director, Charley finds himself an implementer of the worldwide product line managers. Before he had one boss; now he has six, in addition to Nigel Beaumont, who runs a tight fleet and brooks no rebuttal from his captains.

Nigel Beaumont is installing business process reengineering in each of the European subsidiaries. His review team recommends a 12 percent reduction in staff in France. Morale erodes rapidly at High-Liver France. Charley begins to look in earnest. He finds that he is unlikely to be hired by a French company for a French general management position. United Kingdom and

U.S. companies will consider U.S. expatriate general managers for their French subsidiaries, but would prefer to hire French executives. French companies prefer to send French executives to run their U.S. subsidiaries. Beaumont has a director of finance in the UK whom he believes would be an excellent successor for Charley.

Sam Smith then invites Charley back to the United States for a meeting. He recognizes that Charley is uncomfortable with the worldwide product line management system and recommends that Charley round out his international career with an Asian posting to either Indonesia or India. Charley declines, and Sam Smith offers Charley a move back to the United States in a senior staff planning position reporting to Alan Sharp. This will provide an opportunity to work several divisions and subsidiaries of High-Liver and could lead to a transfer opportunity. High-Liver is obligated to move Charley back to the United States, and he concludes that it will be easier to look for a U.S. job from the States. Smith states that the senior staff position tenure will be one year in duration.

Charley Jones lands on his feet. He takes interviews outside the company, but is reclaimed by a division during reorganization. The international division of High-Liver has again been reorganized, and each major division will have a separate and dedicated international operation. Charley is selected as the new vice president and general manager for international operations for the largest and flagship division. He is selected for this position because of his international experience. Alan Sharp leaves High-Liver and joins a major global bank to install a worldwide product management system.

High-Liver is acquired by an investment group, which breaks up the company through a series of divestitures. Charley's division goes through an initial public offering and becomes a public company. Charley is promoted to president and chief operating officer and backup to the chief executive officer. Charley Jones has found a way to a place near the top. It's not exactly as he planned it—but he's there.

Charley Jones is a composite character. All of the events related in this parable actually happened, but not all of them happened in the same sequence to the same person. Let's examine the lessons to be learned from the career-threatening odyssey of Charley Jones:

- First, Charley accepted the challenge of an overseas assignment. He did accept the appointment following some career growth promises from a president two levels up and a human resources manager who failed to brief him on the realities of his new assignment. Second, Charley toughed it out. He whined a little, but settled in to stay the course. Another manager might have cut his losses and run under Marcel Frontenac, demanded an immediate repatriation to the U.S., and settled for a lateral move or downgraded position with High-Liver, or settled for a lesser job with another company.

- Charley Jones developed a marketing plan for his most important product: his own career. He looked at existing markets, new markets, delivery systems, and the composite of his experience. His primary marketing focus remained with his own company, High-Liver. He knew the company's history, its products, and a good part of the political structure. Charley Jones recognized that he must put himself on display without appearing to look for a job.

- Charley maintained his tie lines with the operating divisions of High-Liver. He visited them on his own time and shared his perceptions about the Eastern-bloc marketing opportunities. He became an informal resource to the U.S. divisions relative to product and market opportunities and competitive information. Charley became known to operating executives outside the closed ranks of the president for international operations and his human resource manager accomplice.

- Charley Jones always perceived himself as a fast-moving consumer products industry general manager in waiting, with a strong suit in marketing. He met with the executive search consultants who were willing to give him time, and he gained their perceptions of the marketplace for his skills. He understood that certain industries, such as financial services, credit products, and consumer services offer alternative industries. Charley ruled out the advertising agency segment as a career path early in the building of his career-change plan.

- He negotiated his return home after five years and three relocations (and as many bosses). High-Liver had become an organizationally unstable company. In Charley Jones's case, staying abroad beyond five years would represent risky career planning.

- Charley Jones was been tested by ambiguity and turbulence of a succession of international assignments. He now advises his up-and-comers to take assignments overseas, but to have a clear understanding of when and where they will return.

The current trendline for multinational corporations is to assign staff management positions to local nationals rather than to transfer expatriate managers. Expatriates are generally sent to open up a market and hopefully transition back after a local national manager has been trained. Expatriates also continue to be posted to repair damaged operations. The fixing of an under-performing overseas subsidiary may represent the twilight career step for a senior executive five to ten years from retirement. A soft-landing retirement package may provide an inducement to an old cougar with nothing to lose.

International operations frequently represent more than 50 percent of multinational corporation revenues. Overseas postings provide a management and leadership experience that many times can't be duplicated in a similar U.S. assignment. The opportunities will continue to develop. Many professionals accepting foreign assignments will fail. But those who succeed are likely to have an advantage in the path to the corner office.

NOW YOU'RE SAILING

CROSSING FUNCTIONAL LINES

*Hobson Brown, Jr., President and CEO,
Russell Reynolds Associates*

16

CROSSING FUNCTIONAL LINES

Hobson Brown, Jr., President and CEO,
Russell Reynolds Associates

Both the technological revolution and the globalization of the economy have challenged the organizational flexibility of many larger commercial enterprises. New technologies have enhanced or replaced long-established operational methods. Markets once considered marginal are now being cultivated as a source of future profits. As a result, the factors that once contributed to a business' success are often no longer as influential. Past accomplishments are no longer accurate predictors of future performance.

Over the past decade, senior executives have applied a host of organizational reforms—reengineering, delayering, rightsizing, and so on—to assure the continued prosperity of their companies in an increasingly competitive environment. Furthermore, forward-thinking executives also understand that these reforms have not only led to a relaxation of corporate hierarchies; they have also blurred, (or, in some cases, abolished) many divisions between executive functions. That executives are often required to cross functional lines is now an accepted component of corporate staffing strategy. This trend—as well as the more fluid environment between companies and industries—spells greater opportunities and greater complexity for both those executives pondering a possible cross-functional move and the human resources executives who direct the flow of executive talent.

The Decline of the Functionally Based Career Path

The current corporate career path has its genesis in earlier structures. Indeed, many of today's senior executives entered the workforce at a time when enterprises were geared to achieving a machine-like efficiency. Companies were organized into fairly rigid functional units, such as production, distribution, finance, or sales; executives progressed up the corporate ladder by mastering the skills and responsibilities of their assigned functions.

Yet even during the heyday of "The Organization Man," interaction between functions was frequent, and often necessary. A marketer likely would have to weigh the concerns of the strategic planning department, and a human resources professional would have to include considerations of facilities management when allocating staff. To address the need for cross-functional fluency, management development programs frequently required promising executives to "get their ticket punched" at different divisions as their careers progressed. This laid the foundation for executive moves between staff and line positions. At many major corporations this pattern was fairly standard, and in some cases so much so that it contributed to sub-par performance or premature departures by more than a few otherwise excellent executives. Even so, clear divisions between functions—both between executives on an individual level and corporate divisions on a collective level—would remain the basis for human resource planning.

A host of new realities, many of which were unleashed in the aftermath of the U.S. recession of 1973–1974, forced a major reassessment of corporate structures. The dynamic growth in information technology and its increasing importance as a basic business tool intertwined functional areas by providing a common denominator, in digital form. The implementation of "just-in-time" delivery systems, for example, affected manufacturing, distribution, and sales, blurring the boundaries between them. The globalization of the economy, particularly in the past few years, has dissolved regional boundaries for both marketing and operations. Greater sophistication on the part of both producers and consumers has shortened product and knowledge life cycles. The greatly increased risk of obsolescence and need for agility has raised awareness of the cost, both on an individual and a corporate level, of hewing closely to a functional model.

Beginning in the late 1970s, a response to this trend emerged in the rise of the project-based team, which sought to facilitate innovation and minimize redundancies by increasing the ease by which members of different functional specialties could communicate. A new product launch, for example, would be directed by a team with representatives from research and development to sales, allowing for conflicts to be eliminated while still in the planning stages.

And as the success of such teams helped recast corporate organizational structure, it also helped rewrite the executive career path to include frequent migration between teams founded on project goals instead of function. The team concept more or less brought an end to the purely linear career path. The pressures that challenged corporations—more rapid obsolescence of technology and the greater need for versatile skill sets, for example—filtered down to the individual level. As a result, the ability to cross functional lines is now perceived to be an essential element of career success. In fact, many of today's leading executives have broadly based functional backgrounds.

The acceptance of crossing functional lines is now fully ingrained in conventional wisdom. After all, who could possibly be *against* executives having broader skill sets? Yet this should not obscure the fact that crossing functional lines poses significant challenges, both for executives charting their career paths and those charged with the strategic management of human resources. In contemplating such a move, it is therefore wise to understand the benefits and costs involved to both sides.

Evaluating the Risks and Rewards of a Cross-Functional Move

On the individual level, then, how is an executive to evaluate a potential cross-functional move from, say, divisional controller to an operating division head with profit-and-loss (P&L) responsibility? A number of factors come into play, ranging from the company's strategic priorities to the professional's own set of personal strengths and weaknesses.

First, the move must be considered in relation to one's own level of seniority; both the desirability as well as the feasibility can be affected by where the executive is in his or her career path. A good professional development opportunity, for example, may not make for the best career move. Learning to market a new product may not be worthwhile if doing so will require taking a more junior position in marketing at the moment one is in line for a senior vice-presidency in finance. This issue of "time sensitivity" becomes more important as the corporate pyramid narrows. For example, it is rare for a chief information officer to become corporate chief financial officer. More likely, a divisional chief financial officer will be tapped to head, say, customer service, as part of his or her advancement up the corporate hierarchy. Or the corporate chief financial officer may be awarded P&L responsibility for a large division in order to position him or her as a future candidate for chief executive officer. As a general rule, gathering cross-functional expertise should be done as early as possible in the executive's career, as the opportunities are more numerous near the base of the corporate hierarchy.

It is also important to consider a cross-functional move in relation to the organization's core function—that which defines the company and its mission. This core function (or functions), however, may not always be clear at first glance. Automobile manufacturing companies, for example, often are not led by engineers or manufacturing experts, but by marketing and finance executives—reflecting the underlying importance of market share battles and the considerable capital requirements of that industry. But if the apparent gap between a new position within an organization and that organization's present core function must be examined, it must also be remembered that core functions evolve over time. Witness, for example, the recent strategy of some airlines to shift resources into information services as the area for that industry's greatest future growth. A related factor to be considered is the premium placed within the company on innovation. As a general rule, organizations competing on the basis of efficiency and cost rather than innovation place considerable reliance on functional expertise, as more of their qualitative and quantitative success is drawn from improvements over competitors in sales or distribution or manufacturing.

The process by which an organization advances an individual's career often affects that company's receptivity to the movement of its executives across functional lines. Particular caveats, for example, are warranted for those organizations that promote by direct competition among managers within the same function. Winners of a given competition achieve career advancement, most probably in the form of an increase in the number and nature of their portfolio of responsibilities. Losers, on the other hand, have to await the next "tournament."

An executive within an organization that promotes people in this fashion needs to closely assess how his or her company tolerates failure in such a tournament. The strategic planner who has moved into product marketing might find the lack of his or her functional experience cannot be compensated for by the presence of other, now tangential skills, leading to a lukewarm internal and market response to a new product roll-out. The extent to which one's career would be harmed by such an event must be considered in evaluating the risks of a functional shift.

An individual must also assess the internal situation within the functional area to which he or she might be moving. As fluid as boundaries may be, most functional departments still operate as at least somewhat cohesive groups. If the proposed move fills a vacancy for which others in the department may have been considered, the individual should be prepared to encounter potential political issues. To an extent, an executive in this situation has the vulnerabilities of someone who comes from outside the company to assume a position. The remedies—primarily building trust and teamwork—are the same. But the risks and extra work involved make it appropriate to ask whether assuming such a position offers genuine potential for career growth, or is merely a stopgap solution to an immediate personnel need.

Finally, contemplating crossing functional lines is an opportunity for a frank self-assessment of personal strengths and weaknesses. What are your knowledge gaps and how will you fill them? How long will that take? What is your capacity for continuous learning? What is your appetite for risk? And how will taking this position assist you in fulfilling your ultimate career objectives? In the end, you and you alone are your own best career manager.

The Challenges for Human Resources Executives

Most human resources executives recognize that building an internal executive talent pool with cross-functional expertise helps ensure long-term organizational strength and viability. An individual who has worked as a controller and gone on to assume P&L responsibility as an operating division head will have gained valuable experience on his or her way to becoming CFO, for example—and not only because of a broadened skill set and deeper institutional knowledge: The former controller now sits on the other side of the table, having to manage a business using the financial policies and procedures he or she once instituted.

At the same time, however, cross-functional moves dramatically increase the complexity of human resources management. Both in terms of time and money, the investment in continual professional development can be sizable. Transferring an individual from one functional area to another is a loss of talent by the first group and may well be poorly received by them. Indeed, the potential for resistance is significant. It is difficult to imagine, for example, an operating division head who would, without protest, permit his key lieutenant to move to another division simply because it was good for his subordinate's long-term career planning.

The potential for disequilibrium is great and must be guarded against. Indeed, this is a problem frequently faced by companies that have rotational systems in place to ensure that executives considered as rising stars gain multifunctional expertise. Again, just as the executive who changes departments is in some sense an outsider within his own company, so too does management change within a department make it susceptible to the same vulnerabilities caused by company turnover. This problem is compounded, of course, in a situation where an executive who leaves for one department is replaced not by someone else within that department but with an executive from yet a third area. Building multifunctional expertise cannot take place at the expense of bench strength. This factor, together with succession planning, comprise the key issues that must be confronted when considering the internal impact of executives crossing functional lines.

These issues become more and more sharply focused as the professional moves up the corporate hierarchy toward the chief executive officer position.

While in a less fluid and more predictable functional environment, a small group of executives—even a single individual—might be groomed for the CEO slot, uncertainty as to the requirements of future corporate leadership has led to the necessity of a much larger cohort of potential chief executive officers. Even the term "succession planning" is increasingly being replaced by the term "succession development" to more accurately reflect the nature of the task. The conflict between the need to groom leadership at the functional level and provide top executives with cross-functional experience creates a dilemma that corporations can be expected to struggle with for the foreseeable future.

The cross-functional move presents individuals planning their careers as well as senior-level line and staff executives with a dilemma that has no one-size-fits-all solution. At the same time, it is indisputable that the fundamental nature of executive career development—and of corporate origination structures—has become less and less confined by particular function.

Continued technological change, the globalization of markets, and the ongoing integration of responsibilities through information will continue to fuel this trend, not only from function to function, but from industry to industry and from culture to culture. Thus, despite the challenges it poses, the strategic vision gained by cross-functional adaptability is now the basis not only of corporate prosperity, but also of the success of an individual's executive career.

A New Industry:
The Transferability
of Management Talent

Gerard R. Roche, Chairman, Heidrick & Struggles

A NEW INDUSTRY:
THE TRANSFERABILITY
OF MANAGEMENT TALENT

Gerard R. Roche, Chairman, Heidrick & Struggles

W hen Peter Larson, Johnson & Johnson's top marketing executive, was selected as CEO of sporting goods manufacturer Brunswick Corporation, eyebrows were raised throughout Corporate America. Although Larson had helped J&J expand its product lines worldwide, the switch from headache remedies to bowling balls didn't make sense to many. However, over the last three years, he has helped Brunswick increase market capitalization by almost $2 billion and gross profits by 25 percent. Similarly, the pundits joked when IBM hired Bruce Harreld, president of Boston Chicken, to serve as its chief strategist in 1995. A marketing genius credited with positioning Boston Chicken as a nationwide metaphor for high-quality take-out food, Harreld has revitalized IBM's market position.

These well-publicized executive changes underscore a new reality in Corporate America: Industry expertise is no longer a requirement for many top management positions. In the past, industry knowledge was a necessity for ambitious middle and senior managers. Executives were promoted for their ability to work successfully in a vertical network of customers, suppliers, operations, and processes. Today, as corporations shift gears to radically distinguish themselves from competitors, executives immersed in one industry may be too close to the problems to find breakthrough solutions. On the other hand, a functional specialist in finance, marketing, or other discipline can provide content solutions while bringing an added, valuable dimension.

And remember, in all top management positions, industry and functional expertise are only part of the equation. Emotional intelligence is key. Almost any technical skill can be taught. It's the people skills that earn executives top positions. Executives who work on their people skills can overcome the "label" of almost any industry or functional ghetto.

Trends Shaping Transferability

Transferability is the result of several key trends that have shaped the current economy:

Deregulation.   Managing the evolution from a regulated environment to a deregulated environment typically involves many of the same issues, no matter what the industry happens to be. Working with legislators, infusing a market-oriented mentality in the workforce, and, most important, selling against and outperforming the competition are the key talents necessary for senior and middle management leaders, whether they be in the airline, telecommunications, or energy industries. We have frequently seen executives from the airline industry, one of the first to deregulate, move successfully into positions in telecommunications and other deregulated businesses.

Industry consolidation.   Industry lines are less rigid than they used to be. The Fortune 500 list, which now includes both service and manufacturing companies, reflects the reality that service and manufacturing are becoming increasingly difficult to differentiate. As the lines continue to blur and the business world becomes more complex, executives will no longer fit so neatly into the same boxes as they did in the past. In today's environment, cross-industry recruiting is proliferating as sophisticated companies expect to see a mixed bag of candidates.

Economic growth.   The current job market is the hottest in at least a generation. For professionals and managers, the unemployment rate is less than 2 percent nationwide. At the same time, many companies are challenged to promote from within. Having downsized middle management during the era of reengineering, they face a shortage of executives to promote to senior positions. While most companies prefer leaders who combine functional expertise and industry experience, the shortage of available candidates is forcing them to consider candidates whose background would have been unorthodox 10 years ago.

Major changes in strategy.   More and more companies are looking
   outside their immediate industries for senior-level managers who offer
   a fresh viewpoint or much-needed skills. For example, many heavy-
   manufacturing organizations are following IBM's lead and seeking managers with consumer packaged-goods expertise. Although outsiders
   won't have a deep knowledge of their company and industry, they typically have functional skills that uniquely qualify them to address a current challenge. These skills, combined with an outsider's point of view,
   allow the new executive to bring some breakthrough thinking and market perspective to a company that is often sorely in need of a new perspective. In one of the earliest instances of transferring functional
   talent across industry lines, Apple Computer selected John Sculley,
   Pepsico's top marketing executive, as CEO to shape a new marketing
   strategy. And though Bob Herbold, senior vice president of information
   services and advertising at Procter & Gamble, had spent his entire
   career in the consumer packaged-goods industry, Microsoft recruited
   him to strengthen its consumer marketing efforts and bring discipline
   to its worldwide operations as chief operating officer.

Turnaround situations: Need for radical change in management talent.   For
   many organizations, a change in strategic direction calls for strength-
   ening capabilities in functional areas that were not important in the
   past. While companies know that vision is essential to long term survival, they also understand that leaders with expertise in tactical areas
   like finance can provide innovative operating approaches that drive
   short and medium term profitability. Often, failing companies will
   seek added bench strength by recruiting executives from industries
   that have conducted successful turnarounds. For example, consumer
   products companies have traditionally been strongholds of marketing
   and sales strength, in contrast to telecommunications companies
   that focus on operations or financial services companies that stress
   accounting and finance. We are also seeing service corporations
   recruiting operations managers with IT and "knowledge management"
   expertise.

Mergers and acquisitions.   These transformations, which continue
   unabated in financial services, health care, and other industries, often
   result in the need for specific functional expertise. If executives have
   successfully married two companies, they can often repeat the feat in
   another organization. As interim CEO of Morrison Knudsen, corporate

troubleshooter Steve Miller was the key player in orchestrating a merger with Washington Construction several years ago. Currently, as interim CEO of Waste Management, he is negotiating a merger with US Waste.

Virtual companies.   Temporary "collections" of functional skill sets assembled to accomplish a specific project or address an opportunity are already the modus operandi in entertainment companies and consulting firms. Recognizing the benefits of putting the best functional players together regardless of their "home team," many traditional organizations are already adopting this style of management by forming interdisciplinary teams to direct key projects. Although understanding how to push buttons in a specific company is critical, functional expertise in a project environment is highly transferable. Bob Pittman, formerly chairman and CEO of Six Flags Corporation, a subsidiary of entertainment giant Time-Warner, applied his virtual management skills as CEO of Century 21 Real Estate and is currently doing so as president of America Online.

The final, and possibly the most important trend driving transferability is what some experts call the new employment contract. Executives today face a different playing field than their predecessors. Before the advent of reengineering, downsizing, and restructuring, corporations sought lifetime employees whose commitment was paramount. In turn, executives trusted their employers to develop their careers and protect their tenure. However, reengineering and flattening of the corporate hierarchy have caused a fundamental shift in executive attitudes and behaviors. They have become more willing to change companies, less committed to their present company, and active practitioners of "defensive career management," staying abreast of alternative job prospects even if they have no current intention of changing positions. Experts advise ambitious managers to use their current employer to build functional skills and experience that can help them land a better position at another organization.

Maximizing Your Value

Given the new reality of "managing your own career" and the reality that your company will no longer take care of you in the traditional sense, what are your best options for maximizing your value? How should talented executives manage their careers today? Which functional areas offer the most career leverage? And which skills are more likely to be transferable "tickets to the top" than others?

The skill sets that tend to be most transferable are those that either are somewhat technical, or that can exist as independent disciplines outside the company's unique environment. They are also functions that have a significant impact on generating revenues and saving costs.

Finance. Finance can be a key to the top, particularly in capital-intensive organizations where careful capital allocation, external capital sources, and close financial controls can significantly raise return on assets, which drives stock price. Many companies in the airline, heavy manufacturing, and chemical industries are headed by their former CFOs or by executives who held that position in another industry. In the financial services industry, however, the CFO function is not typically viewed as a track to the top because it is primarily concerned with reporting and control, not capital allocation.

Marketing and sales. Generating revenues is the fundamental principle of almost every private-sector organization. Some, notably consumer packaged-goods companies, have made it a science. The basic principles of targeting customers, and building on brand equity, product positioning, and market research apply not only to cereal but also business-to-business products and conceptual products like news and software. For example, Mark Willes, former vice chairman of General Mills, now serves as chairman, president, and CEO of Times-Mirror Corporation and publisher of the *Los Angeles Times*. Product development, which is often included in the marketing function, is one area that is not especially transferable outside an industry.

Technology. As computers and information management revolutionize how organizations operate, technology executives are taking on new importance. Too often, however, these executives are technically sophisticated but have difficulty viewing their function within the context of the organization's vision and strategy. If technology managers can demonstrate real business savvy and a broad understanding of how technology can position their companies to generate revenues and grow market share, there's a place for them in the senior management ranks. C. Michael Armstrong, who was chairman and CEO at

Hughes Electronics, made a successful transition from an engineering-dominated firm to the consumer-oriented telecommunications industry as chairman and CEO at AT&T.

Management consulting.   The executive suites of Corporate America are filled with the alumni of the major strategy-consulting firms for two major reasons. Typically, partners at a large consulting firm like McKinsey will enter the organization grounded in a discipline like strategic planning, finance, marketing, or one of the hard sciences. And, as consultants, they have been trained ruthlessly to see the big picture. CEOs Lou Gerstner (IBM), Harvey Golub (American Express), and Michael Jordan (CBS) are all veterans of management consulting. But all had tours in other companies before ascending to their current CEO roles.

Functional experts in manufacturing or operations can attain senior management positions within a specific company, particularly if they have revolutionized a manufacturing process or expanded their markets. However, the expertise of most manufacturing experts is confined to their own organization or industry and tends to be product-specific. Roberto Goizueta, CEO of Coca-Cola, was trained as a chemical engineer, but it wasn't his understanding of the soft drink's formula that has made him a hero to shareholders. It was his ability to work with such concepts as economic value added to measure value growth and wealth creation. General Electric CEO Jack Welch and Kodak CEO George Fisher, considered to be among the strongest managers in Corporate America, began their careers as engineers.

Classic staff functions like communications, human resources, and legal can also transfer successfully between industries. However, these positions are not traditionally routes to the top at most organizations because they are viewed as support to the main thrust of business-operations.

When It's Appropriate to Transfer Your Skills

Although transferring industry or functional expertise is a growing trend, it is not always appropriate. If an organization's current CEO has a functional background in marketing, the company will benefit most if the COO comes from a different functional specialty. Diversity of management talent is important to prevent tunnel vision. As legendary airline executive Al Casey says, "You can't have back-to-back levels of ignorance."

Avoid situations where the entire management team consists of industry or functional transfers. Although an outsider's viewpoint can often bring a fresh perspective on organizational challenges, it's important that some insiders have key roles to provide stability and some grounding in reality.

Leveraging your industry or functional expertise requires an honest self-assessment, a willingness to showcase your capabilities, and a commitment to targeting your search. Once you have inventoried your skills and determined your functional expertise, volunteer for large-scale, visible projects that will enable you to demonstrate your abilities to a high level of management. If you are a staff executive with no prospects of ascending the hierarchy, consider a stint as a revenue generator in a consulting firm to demonstrate that you can deal with clients, generate revenues, and manage teams. Or consider a move to the service sector, which accommodates more functional switching than traditional manufacturing typically does.

When you're ready to market yourself outside of your own company, target industries in which your function is a key driver. In capital-intensive businesses, finance executives often rise to the top. In consumer-products companies, marketing is key. And in a growing number of American companies, technology leads the way.

Answering the question of when to transfer your skills is a more elusive challenge. It's important to build functional credibility by paying your dues in a conventional corporate setting before moving on. However, it's also key to move before becoming trapped by your compensation and 401-K plan, or before you become typecast by your company or industry. Generally, we recommend moving on if you have been with your organization for more than four years without being promoted.

Your career path is not entirely under your own control. While vertical careers—those that begin and end in the same industry—are still the norm for the majority of corporate executives, many companies are looking outside their industry for senior level managers. Be sure to explore opportunities that may unexpectedly present themselves. A call from an executive search firm, a lead from a friend, or a tip from your active network can lead to an important career boost or transition that you hadn't considered.

REACHING YOUR DESTINATION

EVALUATING THE JOB OFFER

Steven B. Potter, Managing Partner,
Highland Search Group

Evaluating the Job Offer

Steven B. Potter, Managing Partner,
Highland Search Group

The interviews are over. You are exhilarated and a little anxious, for you are expecting a job offer imminently. Now comes the hard part. What should you do now? To whom should you turn for advice? What do you ask?

Most job search candidates assume that the receipt of an offer spells the end of the search process—that the next steps will be straightforward and uneventful. Nothing could be further from the truth. It is generally at the offer stage that Murphy's Law takes over, and all sorts of expectations and hopes get dashed. Assessing an offer, even if it is for a dream job, requires a mix of sobriety, and skepticism, and a touch of Machiavelli. After all, it is your life and your career that will be most affected.

Negotiating the offer should be viewed as an extension of your interviews. How you are perceived during these final stages, while not as critical as the initial interview sessions, will influence how you are perceived once you join your new employer. Striking the delicate balance between securing yourself the best deal and not appearing to be too adversarial or headstrong is paramount in the negotiation process.

At the Highland Search Group, which specializes in financial services, we have had the opportunity to negotiate hundreds of contracts at all levels, from chief executive officer to junior analyst. The following is a primer on what to consider during the job offer negotiations. While it is not comprehensive, it accounts for the elements common to all job negotiations as well as important details that crop up in most offer letters. Because our field of expertise is in financial services recruiting, our comments should, at a minimum, be taken as food for thought. Outside the rarefied atmosphere of the executive suite or Wall Street, most employees are lucky enough to get offer letters. Other than the workforces within unions or public service sectors, the vast majority of employees do not have contracts, much less job security.

Starters

The first rule of thumb in considering any offer is to be sure that you actually want the job. It is tempting to use job offers to leverage your current position or to send your boss a message that you are not being properly appreciated. In the hot industries of the 1990s, such as technology and finance, the repercussions of this "stalking horse" strategy rarely backfire because it is so widely anticipated. But while it is flattering to become the subject of a bidding war, this should not become a habit. Your interest in receiving an offer from another employer should be based on good faith—that there is at least some expectation that you will take the job if the terms make sense to you.

Assuming that you are serious about your pending offer, you should then ask as many questions as possible, trivial though they may seem, before you receive an offer in writing. Make sure that you have ironed out all of the big issues such as compensation, length of agreement, job responsibilities, reporting lines, title, and benefits before you ask for the offer letter. Complete your due diligence on your future employer and ensure that you have had the opportunity to ask difficult questions about your career path, your new colleagues, and your new bosses. Seek out alumni of the organization who can give you honest feedback on their experiences. Nothing irritates hiring managers and human resources professionals more than having to rewrite several drafts of an offer letter, especially when the changes seem picayune. The element of surprise in the final negotiations is usually unwelcome.

Give yourself a time limit on your decision, or your future employer will do it for you. Sitting on a firm offer for too long gives people the impression that you are stalling, or indecisive, or that you are shopping your offer around to other employers. While you should feel free to investigate all opportunities, do not make a company go to the trouble of making an official offer until you are fairly sure you are ready to make the jump.

The Recruiter's Role

Recruiters play an invaluable role in the offer negotiation process. In fact, much of the value a search firm adds to the recruiting exercise rests in its facilitating the negotiation. You should be aware, however, that most if not all search firms are paid by the hiring client and therefore represent their client's interests. This does not mean that the recruiter will be insensitive to your concerns, but the recruiter is not your personal agent.

Good recruiters treat both sides at the negotiating table as equals and will endeavor to strike a fair deal for both the candidate and the client. To the extent that you trust the recruiter, you should take him into your confidence, because the more information you give the better the recruiter will be able to balance your interests with those of his client. So, while the recruiter's financial interests are technically aligned with his client, he is also well aware that making you happy in the recruiting process will help ensure a lasting relationship between you and your future employer.

The Lawyer's Role

Lawyers should be heard and not seen, and certainly not seen by your new employer. While it is important to have a legal expert evaluate the language of your contract, especially if there are technical points that seem confusing, it is best to keep your lawyer out of direct negotiations and in the background. Your lawyer should only be brought into the picture when the deal is basically done. Of course, in high-level negotiations (particularly, in sports, where lawyers often serve as agents), the lawyers do all the talking and hammer out the deal. But, for executives (except at the president or CEO level), part of your continuing appeal will result from your appearance of negotiating for yourself and making your own decisions. And if your lawyer takes center stage, you may run the risk of appearing too adversarial and unyielding just at the moment when you should be projecting trust and good faith.

If you choose to have a lawyer represent you, try to find one that specializes in employment law. General practitioners or legal experts in other fields, even if they are your neighbors or college friends, will not have the experience with employment contracts necessary to provide constructive advice. Without expert attention, you may become frightened and even more confused, causing distrust to settle in your mind and the deal to crater potentially. Employment lawyers who have negotiated many contracts know what to look for. They can recognize what is standard boilerplate language and what is unusual or rare or even onerous and unfair. Because the threat of litigation raises a specter over all employers, many contracts are written in legal jargon, sometimes running to 20 pages or more. Even the more colloquial versions contain numerous legal concepts. Your lawyer's ability to cut through the verbiage and hone in on the important issues will save you time and anxiety.

The Offer Letter

Before you break out the champagne and toast the future, there is the matter of the offer letter. It is the crucial document that defines your role and protects your interests. Everyone, even the most junior professional, is entitled to some letter outlining the job responsibility, compensation, benefits, and other matters. Many letters, however, tend to include only basic details, and this is often sufficient for junior-level employees.

In the best cases, offer letters should be seen once and never needed again. Or, to put it another way, if you have to reread your offer letter later on, you know that you are in trouble. Offer letters should be uncontroversial—merely a record of your oral agreement, to be tucked away in your filing cabinet.

Termination Provisions

Offer letters, even lengthy ones, generally devolve into three key components: your job security, what you will get, and what happens if you leave the company. The last part is what senior executives spend the most time (and the most of their lawyer's time) examining, especially during these uncertain times of downsizing and merger activity. Not surprisingly, the bulk of most offer letters for senior executives deals with various termination provisions, such as what happens if you are fired or laid off. Most employers have devoted considerable energy to committing to paper practical provisions in their termination language. Each firm may use slightly different language to encompass the same definitions. Employees and employers both generally feel it is helpful to deal with what happens at the end of employment at the beginning of the negotiations. Rather than being scared off by this, you should use it to your advantage.

Legal employment status varies from state to state. Under New York State law, for instance, all employees are employed at will—which means that either you or your employer can sever your relationship at any time and for any reason. There is no statute governing this law, as it is grounded in common law (with roots that go back to the drafting of the Magna Carta). This small clause essentially changes the deal from an employment contract to a compensation agreement, specified for a certain term. For this reason, it is important to note that, unless stated in writing or orally, you are not guaranteed employment under any circumstances, only entitled to bonuses and other benefits under the term of the contract. You should determine whether you do, in fact, have some job security under your contract, and you should check with your lawyer to confirm whether it is enforceable.

The termination provisions are usually divided into two main clauses: for cause and without cause. In the first case, the employer reserves the right to fire you without further compensation or benefits (other than mandatory health insurance coverage) under a variety of scenarios that would deem you dangerous or unfit for employment at the company.

"Cause" is generally defined as constituting:

- A criminal act (misdemeanor or felony) under Federal law
- Violation of self-regulatory laws or rules
- An act of fraud or major act of dishonesty detrimental to the standing of your firm's reputation
- Violation of firm policies
- Gross or willful negligence, misconduct, or insubordination
- Engaging in a conflict of interest
- Inability to perform your job for some specified period of time (as a result of death or disability)

Other definitions of cause that have worked their way into offer letters include illegal drug usage or sale, and sexual misconduct. Importantly, companies only reserve the right to terminate you on these grounds: they are not required to. In the case of minor infractions, many companies offer the ability to "cure" the problem within a month and are generally bound to give you fair written notice before taking any punitive actions.

Many of the definitions of cause seem like common sense and force you merely to abide by fairly basic ethical guidelines. For the most part, you would do well not to argue for changes, since these definitions are set in stone and are considered corporate policy. In one case, we spent four weeks negotiating a deal solely on the definition of cause, where our candidate's lawyer debated endlessly with our client on what constituted fraud (was it proven fraud or alleged fraud?). While these were certainly valid legal points to discuss in a different forum, the hiring manager nearly threw in the towel, and the candidate might have lost a great opportunity. It pays to see the forest for the trees.

You should ask for language, even if it seems redundant, that describes what happens if you are terminated without cause. In the best case, you will receive or vest all monies and other compensation (stock, options, deferred funds) on an accelerated basis, so that you are untethered from your firm immediately. In the worst instance, you might be forced to stay on the premises until the term of your contract has expired to receive what is due you. This seems blatantly unfair to the employee, but employers use it as a bullying tactic to evade paying out bonuses, guaranteed or not. Either way, it is important to have the basic terms of separation spelled out in advance to avoid unpleasant surprises.

Many senior executives often ask for language that allows them to leave their jobs for cause, a feature commonly known as resignation with cause. In this case, certain events need to take place for the executive to exercise this option. Usually, a change of control (via a merger), a material diminishment of the executive's duties, or a serious default by the company of its obligations represent sufficient grounds to resign one's position. These are contentious issues in the negotiation process, since companies do not want to inhibit the scope of their corporate activities (mergers) or lose the right to replace or demote an executive who does not perform. Nevertheless, it is widespread enough at the highest levels that it has become expected practice.

Arbitration Provisions

After the termination provisions, the next most critical sections of most offer letters deal with legal recourse on disputes and noncompete restrictions. In the former, many companies, especially securities firms, seek to have all legal disputes subject to arbitration, rather than a court trial. In the main, this has been a positive development for both sides, since arbitrations tend to be quicker and cheaper than full-blown jury trials. The acceptance of your offer, therefore, binds you to arbitration and the waiver of any court action. Your comfort level with this decision will depend on your view of the arbitration process but is not something that should get in the way of making your decision to join your new employer.

Noncompete Covenants

Noncompete restrictions are designed to prevent an employee from using harmful information or committing deleterious actions that would damage the employee's company meaningfully. In most cases, the restrictive covenants enjoin a former employee from poaching other employees, or using confidential, nonpublic information for the benefit of a competitor, or soliciting clients of your former firm. It is important to examine the scope of the noncompete restrictions, since it is possible that they could be so severe as to make it impossible to secure another job. Generally noncompete restrictions that essentially block all future employment opportunities are unlikely to be held up by a court and should be deemed unacceptable on principle. Nonetheless, most restrictive covenants typically remain in force for one year after an employee is terminated, whether for cause or without cause. For some, especially in the latter case (without cause), this seems unfair, but it is common enough to take notice of it. The laws regarding restrictive covenants are complex and vary from state to state, so you should check with your lawyer before agreeing to any restrictions. At the least, you should negotiate the terms of any restrictive covenants before you accept an offer, and ask ahead of time if there will be any expectation of signing a noncompete document *after* you have already started your new job.

Mitigation Clauses

Another matter that crops up in some offer letters is the so-called "no mitigation" clause. This provision prevents employers from withholding or reducing previously guaranteed compensation of a terminated employee (without cause) in the event the employee gets another job before the contract expires. Under this clause the employer will not be allowed to offset payments for the exact amount earned by the employee at a different job. Without this clause, some employers even require that the terminated employee seek employment or attempt to reduce the payments owed to the employee. Clearly the employer is trying to avoid paying out monies since, it could be argued, the employee will enjoy the benefit of double compensation. On Wall Street, the absence of this clause (or the inclusion of its opposite) is nearly universally damned as being unfair to the employee, in that it punishes him for doing no wrong if he is laid off during the term of his contract. It also violates the spirit of the original contract and the notion of a guarantee in the first place. Outside of Wall Street, mitigation is taken for granted; the offset is expected. Try during your negotiations to get the "no mitigation" clause inserted (though, unless you are a senior investment banker, it is not likely you will prevail).

Minor Points

Other points to look for in standard offer letters include:

Rights of assignment.   This section, generally a sentence at most, calls for any successor firm or acquirer to respect and honor the terms of your original contract.

Duties.   Your job responsibilities should be spelled out in as much detail as is necessary.

Term.   This is important for obvious reasons but it also generally marks the limits of the noncompete covenants.

Indemnification.   Senior executives, more often than not, receive language in their contracts agreeing to hold them harmless against liability (under the relevant state laws) for services rendered under the scope of his employment. More junior executives should not expect to see this clause in their letters.

Drug test.   Some employers (again especially on Wall Street) require all employees to be tested for illegal drug usage before an offer letter becomes valid. The only advice we can give you is stay off poppy-seed bagels for a few days, because the seeds sometimes show up as opium in the test.

Final Tips

Despite the often arduous task of negotiating an offer, you should not let the details overshadow the big picture. Ask yourself always why you are doing this, and what interests you in this opportunity. Be flexible where you can. Concede the small points in return for potentially bigger rewards. At some point, the negotiating will have to come to an end and you will have to make a leap of faith. For it is not a letter that will provoke a job change—it is the new people you will work with and the career improvement that will push you over the edge.

MAKING SENSE OUT OF DOLLARS: HOW TO NEGOTIATE A COMPENSATION PACKAGE

John F. Johnson, Chairman,
LAI Ward Howell

MAKING SENSE OUT OF DOLLARS: HOW TO NEGOTIATE A COMPENSATION PACKAGE

John F. Johnson, Chairman,
LAI Ward Howell

The phone rings one evening. Out of the blue you are presented with a new career opportunity that will offer you more responsibility, an impressive new title, the opportunity for advancement, and the way out of an employment situation that has grown stale. So begins a series of events that will involve interviews, reference checks, individual soul searching, family dialogues, and possibly an eventual offer to join a new employer. This scenario could also involve the opportunity to move to a new assignment within your existing company, but more often than not it involves setting off into new territory and embarking on a new leg in your professional journey.

Negotiating the compensation package is usually the final event in the process of assessing a new career opportunity. It is important that professionals considering changing jobs don't put the cart before the horse. Moving into the wrong job for a great compensation package almost always leads to a second move within a reasonably short period of time. Therefore, assessing the job fit with one's interests, skills, and long-term career objectives should all come before negotiating and evaluating the offer the new employer might make to you.

Coming to terms on the specific provisions of an offer can be very difficult, especially at the senior levels of management. Negotiating today's increasingly intricate compensation packages requires the tact of a concierge and the delicate hand of a surgeon. However, there are a few basic guidelines to keep in mind during the process.

Some Basic Guidelines

First and foremost, the higher the level of job within the company, the greater the ability of a candidate to negotiate on compensation. Remember your first job as a teenager? It probably paid the minimum wage, maybe with a few token extras thrown in. As a rule, entry-level workers have little ability to alter their proffered terms of employment. Most compensation packages at this level focus strictly on salary, bonus, and benefits. That is, unless you are one of the highly sought-after MBAs from Harvard or Stanford, who in today's world are being fought over by the likes of McKinsey, Booz Allen, or the Microsoft and Intels of the world.

As one rises up the corporate ladder, compensation packages become larger and more complex with every successive rung. Therefore, the ability to negotiate unique compensation packages becomes greater as the job titles become loftier. At the very highest levels—CEOs, COOs, and CFOs—the negotiations can involve all of the complexity of an international trade treaty, complete with provisos, codicils, and addenda. The disclosure forms that publicly-held companies file with the Security and Exchange Commission are filled with arcana about top executives' compensation packages.

A second general concept to keep in mind is that your employer's ability and willingness to negotiate varies in inverse proportion to the company's size. The largest companies will tend to negotiate very little. Smaller companies, by contrast, are more likely to engage in negotiating trade-offs even for lower-level employees. When offered a job at a small website development firm you are more likely to deal closely with the owner, founder, or chief executive, who has a great deal of discretion when it comes to putting together compensation packages. By contrast, human resources executives at Fortune 500 companies generally operate within a corporate framework. For General Motors to negotiate separate job offers for each of its 300,000 employees is just not feasible.

Whether you are a sports agent or used-car buyer, a common rule of negotiation holds that the first person to mention a figure loses. Generally, prospective employers will not ask how much you would like to make, or how much or little it will take to get you to sign on. But if asked to name a figure, candidates could respond by saying they expect to be paid as much as others in the same job classifications; or they could use their current salary as a benchmark simply by stating "current base, bonus, and other key compensation factors." If a search consultant is involved, his role is to bring you and your prospective employer together, and he will most likely have provided the client with your compensation history. There is a good chance the person sitting across the table will know exactly how much you are currently making.

First of all, never accept a job without knowing the details of the offer, from salary to benefits. However, several factors may make it difficult to do so. In the excitement of receiving what may seem to be an attractive opportunity, the instinct is often to simply say yes. Or, you may feel pressured to reach a decision quickly, especially if some sort of personal relationship exists, or has developed, between you and the hiring manager.

It is important to you as a new employee to know exactly what you are getting into. The strongest negotiating position you have is when the company has decided that you are its leading candidate and wants to move forward with an offer. It is okay to indicate a strong level of interest, but it should always be understood that any formal acceptance of a job offer is contingent on the financial package being acceptable to both parties.

Striking the Right Tone

It is always important to strike the right tone when entering into negotiations. Potential employees intent on playing hardball run the risk of starting the relationship off on the wrong foot. A common mistake is to believe that you have more leverage than you actually possess. It is true that with the unemployment rate hovering at 20-year lows, the labor market *is* tight, especially in particular professions and regions. Desirable skill sets have never commanded such a premium. In fact, so-called middle managers, those just below the level of vice president, are becoming more valued and integral members of the corporate staff. With the flattening of organizations and constant restructurings, fewer direct reports now separate line managers from the executive suite. Between 1985 and 1995, for example, General Electric slashed its layers of management from seven to three. As middle managers are entrusted with more responsibility, firms have proven more willing to commit more resources to finding potential hires. Last year alone, searches for general managers below the division-head level rose 58 percent.

It's more likely now than ever in the past that you will receive a call from a headhunter. But just because you receive an offer after being reeled in by a search consultant doesn't mean that you are the only candidate being considered, or the only one deemed qualified for the position. Recruiters who take their job seriously present a list of viable candidates to the employer. Therefore, while walking away from the table may be one of the oldest and most daring negotiating tactics, it won't necessarily get you what you are seeking. The chances are that someone else is waiting in the wings.

Rather than simply making demands, it's important to start negotiating the compensation package by asking questions. You are entitled to know as much as possible about the job, the organization, and the compensation range, just as the company is going to find out as much as possible about you.

Compensation Package Components

Let's look at the components of a compensation package and what can and cannot be negotiated. For lower-level positions, expect a salary and bonus and not much in the way of negotiating room. Higher-level positions normally will have a salary, bonus, equity participation, and other long-term incentives. Such inducements previously made up a small portion of a compensation offer but today are assuming greater prominence. Whereas middle managers might find 80 percent of their cash compensation in salary, at more senior management levels the salary will account for significantly less than 50 percent of total pay.

When it comes to negotiating base salary, consider the following. Many companies have compensation ranges for particular positions with varying levels of experience. Find out what the range is for your job, either from the human resources officer or the recruiter, and go from there. If a company is unwilling to share that information, there is reason for concern. For instance, if you're currently a marketing manager making $95,000, and the range for the marketing director position is $80,000 to $125,000, you know that to get a meaningful increase you will be pushing yourself near the top of the range.

Anecdotal press reports to the contrary, most new-hires do not receive sign-on bonuses. For oil engineers, software writers, web designers, and other professionals currently at a high point in the demand cycle, these bonuses become commonplace. But a director of financial planning leaving one Fortune 500 company for another is unlikely to receive a sign-on bonus just for agreeing to take a new post.

Annual bonuses are prevalent almost in all industries. But again, they can be difficult to negotiate, especially outside the normal ranges that companies have established. If operations go according to plan, the company normally will pay out a fixed amount in bonuses. If the business unexpectedly flounders or oversucceeds, the bonus plans pay out nothing or drive target. At lower levels, bonuses are more discretionary and based upon the assessment of an individual's manager. If an executive has profit responsibility, however, the bonus will most often be tied to the performance of that business. The higher someone rises in a corporation, the more that individual's bonus is tied to the firm's overall performance. Indeed, for those at the very top, bonuses are normally tied to issues beyond the control of any one individual, such as the performance of the company's stock or other external benchmarks.

Those at the executive level do have some negotiating power when it comes to bonuses. This is especially true if taking a new position at midyear means leaving behind an accrued bonus with an employer. This is common on Wall Street for analysts, traders, investment bankers, and other managers. In the financial world, where bonuses constitute the lion's share of compensation, leaving Paine Webber for J. P. Morgan in August may disqualify a public relations manager from participating in the bonus pool at his old firm. Therefore, companies are willing to guarantee bonuses for the new recruit.

Executives of all types, and in all fields, are finding that option grants are assuming a greater prominence in their compensation packages. Once the exclusive domain of top-level executives, equity opportunity is being driven down to significantly lower levels in most organizations to stimulate a sense of ownership and loyalty.

The Growing Prominence of Stock Options

CEOs in industries ranging from steel to software are enlisting their employees as fellow shareholders. In the last year, 90 percent of the compensation packages garnered by LAI candidates included some kind of equity participation. For those at the highest job levels, 100 percent received options. For those in midrange posts, 75 percent did. Such grants can, in fact, prove to be increasingly valuable. In a recent trend analysis, Pearl Meyer & Partners, a compensation firm, reported that equity pay accounts for the bulk of the gain in total management compensation. For those occupying the executive suite, fixed salaries as a percentage of total compensation have declined significantly in recent years.

Joe Nacchio, formerly head of AT&T's long-distance unit, received options on an estimated 10 million shares when he accepted the top post at the tiny telecommunications start-up Qwest Communications International. The mammoth grant was offered in part to compensate Nacchio for the risk inherent in leaving a top job at one of America's oldest and most venerable firms for a company in its infancy, and in part to compensate him for the large amount of AT&T options he was forced to leave behind.

If signing on with a new firm means leaving a substantial amount of stock options unexercised, you should be able to negotiate either an upfront option grant or cash in lieu of the cash left behind. Executives who possess options should therefore make a calculation as to their worth before entering into salary negotiations. Your new employer will need to keep this issue in mind in order to make the transition worthwhile. Since the value of options in packages varies widely according to an individual's expertise, this is an issue that can definitely be negotiated.

It is important to keep options in perspective, however. With the long-running bull market of the 1990s, which has showed the stamina of a marathon runner, the investing public seems to have forgotten that stocks can, indeed, slide over long periods of time. Anyone who has options should realize that he is at the mercy of the stock market and that the value could fluctuate either way.

Once salary, bonus, and equity issues have been clarified in a compensation offer, there are still a number of areas in which candidates may have the opportunity to negotiate. Some companies will offer perks such as automobiles, club memberships, and financial consulting. These types of perks, however, are currently being squeezed at all levels. Car allowances and clubs are going to a smaller group of people. Other components of a package may offer similarly little room for negotiation. For instance, if a company has a 401(k) or profit-sharing program, all employees will be eligible. That is not negotiable.

Relocation costs are also generally included in the compensation package. If accepting a job means uprooting a family, selling a house, packing worldly belongings into a truck, and shipping them more than 3,000 miles across country, the employee may have some room for negotiations. For instance, interim housing or general travel allowances will often be thrown in to make a difficult process easier.

The last, and perhaps least-contemplated portion of any compensation package is severance. Severance packages are a little like life insurance. They are necessary to have and they might come in handy, but it's uncomfortable to contemplate their use. Lately some massive severance packages have become front-page headlines. When Michael Ovitz was driven out of the number-two slot at Disney in 1997, he went home with options and severance pay worth up to $90 million by some accounts. However, such controversial and massive packages are aberrations. Most companies have severance policies that call for six months to one year of salary continuance. It is always of value to understand what normal policy is; but making an issue of negotiating outside traditional policy may often be a red flag to your new employer.

Relying on Executive Recruiters

When negotiating a compensation offer, it is natural to confide in and rely on the executive recruiter for help. But keep in mind that the employer is compensating the search consultant. However, it is in the best interest of the consultant to assist in negotiating a fair and equitable compensation package so that both the employer and new employee are happy about their decision to come together. Therefore, candidates should feel comfortable in asking recruiters anything they want to about company pay policies.

Good recruiters want to be heavily involved in the negotiation of the final package. The higher up you go, the more involved the recruiter is going to be in making each party understand what is important to the other. At the top levels, ideally the recruiter is the intermediary until the candidate is willing to accept the offer. Recruiters view their role as the liaison between the realistic expectations and reasonable objectives of both parties.

Candidates often ask for other potential sources of help in evaluating an offer. There are firms that specialize in the increasingly complex world of compensation consultation, although they are primarily oriented toward working with corporations, not individuals. Their services can be expensive, and they do not negotiate on behalf of executives. Those top-level executives looking for assistance with negotiations, and especially complex ones involving detailed contracts, will normally use the services of attorneys who have significant experience in employment contracts. While such professional services are expensive, there are free resources to which many employees can turn.

With every year, more studies about banding and compensation within specific industries are being published. Trade publications such as CFO *magazine*, or magazines geared toward human resources, contain useful data on compensation within those functions. Other sources are available to assist executives in other functional or industry areas in assessing their worth.

In closing, negotiating a compensation offer is the culmination of what, hopefully, has been a well thought out assessment of the fit between the hiring company and the prospective employee. Assuming that both sides have done a thorough evaluation, the arrival at an agreeable compensation arrangement is normally a relatively easy matter. The higher the level of the individual, the more complex the issues and the more value a search consultant brings to the process. But if you recognize that thousands of employment offers are being extended and accepted daily, it becomes clear that rational minds win out, and that employees will move into new assignments with appropriate rewards.

20

THE FINAL TASK: INTEGRATING INTO YOUR NEW COMPANY

Gary S. Goldstein, President, The Whitney Group

THE FINAL TASK: INTEGRATING INTO YOUR NEW COMPANY

Gary S. Goldstein, President, The Whitney Group

The interviewing is over. An offer has been made and you have accepted it. Now on the job at your new company, you want to be successful. In order to do so, you must get to know the company and integrate into its structure. And whether you realize it or not, you started that process while you were interviewing for your new position. That's because "integrating" is about building relationships—with the company and with the people who work for it.

Break the Ice

You build those relationships the same way you build any relationship you care about. Slowly. Carefully. First, you get a sense of the chemistry between you and the people you meet. You show your human side and get to know your new associates on both a personal and a professional level. You discover if you share similar goals, or—at the very least—if your goals are compatible. Remember: Relationships are living, breathing organisms that grow over time. Don't rush the ones you have at your new job; nurture them.

When you start a new job, you usually have a three- to six-month "honeymoon" during which you must let people get to know you. Don't isolate yourself; spend time with your coworkers. Instead of waiting for them to come to you, bring them into your world. Volunteer for projects that would benefit from your skills. (But beware, don't become overzealous. Do what fits into the style of the organization.) Participate in internal seminars and classes where the skills of the participants will be mixed differently from the way they would in a traditional office situation. Go to every party and social event, and use them as a way to build personal relationships.

The perils of failing to do so can be illustrated by David's story. David was recruited by a small, privately held investment firm for a new position in the organization. He and the 70-year-old president and founder hit it off during the interview process, and they continued to get along during the first few months that David was on the job. David worked hard at meeting his responsibilities and building relationships with key office managers around the country, but he was determined to keep his business and social lives separate. He didn't go to the company's holiday party or to its summer picnic. He seemed to have the attitude that these events were boondoggles.

In October, the president held the company's annual fall get-together at his country home. David, facing the beginning of a long cross-country business trip the next day, skipped the party. The president had already begun to question David's commitment to the company. He had been concerned when David missed the two earlier events; he thought David's absence showed a lack of interest in the human side of the company. Now in the wake of the October party, he was convinced that David wasn't willing to be part of the company family. Within two weeks of David's return from the business trip, he and the president were discussing a severance package.

Remember Your Supporters

When you interview for a new position, make sure that you meet the key people with whom you'll be dealing. If you're certain that they are on-board about you before you accept the job, you know that they will be your biggest boosters. You know that once you are on the job, they will want you to succeed so that their good opinion of you will be confirmed. They will be eager to help you—from providing you with the resources you need to introducing you to other members of the organization. But don't take your supporters for granted. Keep them up to date about your activities. For example, once a quarter, schedule lunch or breakfast with each of them just to talk and exchange ideas.

Build Your Credibility

Many people make the mistake of jumping into their new jobs with both feet. They criticize everything the company does and offer dozens of unsolicited opinions. They end up taking a politically incorrect position or suggesting an idea that has already been tried and failed. Behave this way and you will alienate yourself from your coworkers and the rest of the organization.

Instead, sit back, listen, and observe. Get to know the dynamics of the organization. Participate in as many internal meetings as you can. Speak with people throughout the company and ask lots of questions. Look for practical ways for the company to improve business. Make sure that you collect enough data to make intelligent observations and creative suggestions.

Relationships flourish in an environment of give and take, where each person recognizes that the other has reasons for what he or she does. In biding your time and doing your fact-finding, you will demonstrate your respect for others and will be more credible when you *do* speak. And when you do, be diplomatic. If you need to criticize, frame your comments within your personal experience so that they do not come across as judgmental.

Make a Contribution

First impressions are lasting impressions. When you are hired, other members of the organization assume that you have something to contribute to the business. Waste no time in making all the contributions you can. Even if what you do doesn't shake the world, you will still develop a great reputation as a doer, as someone of value to the organization.

Take the story of Phyllis, for example. Phyllis second-guessed herself about taking her new job. She could do much of the work in her sleep, she told herself, and new opportunities were probably two or three years in the future. But the job came with a significant salary increase, and it was in a fast-growing division of a large insurance company. She decided to accept the offer. Within three months of her arrival, she had produced two marketing brochures, materials for which the sales force had been begging. The brokers called her boss to thank him for hiring her. By her first anniversary, she had doubled the number of sales tools available to the field and had launched a monthly newsletter that not only kept the sales force up-to-date on business issues in the division but was being imitated by others in the company. Phyllis was well-rewarded: She received a record bonus for a first-year employee, and the opportunities that she had thought were at least another year away suddenly started presenting themselves.

Remember, if you don't live up to your promise—if you have nothing to deliver within the first three to six months, you may be seen as a failure. It's an image that is almost impossible to shake. Just as you would become distrustful in a personal relationship if your partner didn't keep his or her promises, so too will your coworkers.

Know Your Limits

Before you accept a job offer, make sure that the boundaries of your responsibilities are clearly defined and that you know how your success will be measured. Then, don't overstep those limits. Take on more than you should, and you will be perceived as a power-monger with grandiose ideas. You will create a bad impression that is difficult to overcome. Find out how your predecessors were seen by the organization, and what they did right and what they did wrong. Learn from their mistakes. In all good relationships, the parties know their responsibilities and respect the limits that others set.

It is also important to communicate with the organization as a whole. An internal news release that you review and approve can explain who you are, what you will be doing, and why. This tactic is especially valuable if your job is a new position at the company. Then go out and meet people—not to evaluate them but to find out if there is anything you can do to assist them. You will learn a great deal because you will have put people at ease right away. By showing them that you are there to help them, you will prove yourself to be a partner, not an adversary, and they will feel comfortable about sitting down and talking with you.

Join the Team

Whatever you do in your new job, always send the following message: "We are in this together." Be nonthreatening. You want your managers, coworkers, and direct reports to feel that you have the best interests of the company—and them—at heart. Show them how they can benefit from whatever you are doing. Even if you came in to execute a turnaround, make it clear that while you know that all your decisions may not be popular, your job is to help the company. The health of the company, after all, will ensure that people continue to have jobs, draw paychecks and build their careers.

Find a Mentor

A mentor can be a valuable asset to your career at a company. However, a successful mentoring relationship is just that—a relationship. When selecting a mentor, make sure she or he is someone with whom you are simpatico. Do you click? Do you have compatible interests both personally and professionally? Is there a common link between you? During the interview process, you may already have identified potential candidates. Once at your new company, you should explore every possibility, looking for someone you like and who likes you. Have breakfast or lunch with people and find out whether there is any chemistry between you.

Consider Roger. He landed his second job out of college at a broker-dealer as one of three junior traders in the company's new fixed-income department. Roger was friendly and outgoing. The department's managing director was quiet and introverted. But the 25-year age difference and their personalities didn't stop them from liking each other. Why? Because they found they shared a passion for entrepreneurship; they were both excited about building a new business for the company. Then they discovered another common interest: golf. Roger tried to have lunch with the managing director at least once a month, and the two of them began playing golf together at corporate conferences.

Two years later, when the fixed-income department's business had exploded and the staff had tripled, Roger was asked to manage the trading desk. He had limited experience, but the managing director was comfortable with him, appreciated his enthusiasm, and recognized his abilities. Now the two of them had lunch more frequently. They also played golf twice a month on the weekends, then spent the afternoon discussing the business and ways to build it. As a result, when the managing director was promoted, Roger got a new job running what was now a major profit center. Roger's choice of a mentor was someone who could teach him *and* someone he liked and with whom he shared interests. The relationship allowed him to leverage his career and reach a position he might not have reached for another 5 to 10 years.

A cautionary note: Be careful not to choose a mentor based only on the person's political strength in the organization. Some strong political animals are controversial and are not well-liked. If you pursue a relationship with one, you may be linked with that person when or if he or she falls. Make sure that you understand where someone fits into the organization before you attach yourself to him or her.

Manage Your Individual Relationships

Just as there are subtle differences in how you manage relationships with people you care about—your parents, your friends or your spouse—so there should be differences in how you relate to people at different levels in your new company. When you manage up, be aware at all times that senior people need to see you as an asset, someone of value to them in their own careers. Be supportive, provide good intelligence, and show them that you are on their team. You want them to look on you as someone they can take along as they rise in the organization, perhaps even as a successor.

Within your peer group, be nonthreatening. Be a member of the team, not the boss of it. Compliment your peers when they deserve it. When offering criticism, make it constructive so that you will be perceived as helpful. With junior staff, demonstrate that while you are the authority, you are not there to police them or keep track of how often they screw up. Remain open and available so that those junior to you will not be intimidated. Be approachable so that they can come to you to get the resources and support they need to do their jobs. The more successful they are, the more successful you are.

Map Out Your Future

You have a new position today, but you should also be looking ahead. Think about your career path and where you want to be in five years. After you've been on the job for a few months, start introducing yourself to the people who can help you get where you want to go. Tell them that you are interested in what they do and that you want to learn about it. Start an informal dialogue over lunch from time to time. But whatever you do, make sure your activities are not misconstrued. It wouldn't do for you to give anyone the impression that only months into a new job, you are already looking for your next position. Your investigations should be seen as information-gathering—another way you are learning about the company and how its divisions function, so that you can better integrate into the organization.

21

So You Want to Be a Top Executive? Here's What It Takes

Dennis C. Carey, Vice Chairman,
Spencer Stuart, U.S.

So You Want to Be a Top Executive? Here's What It Takes

Dennis C. Carey, Vice Chairman,
Spencer Stuart, U.S.

More than 10 years of recruiting senior executives for the world's top corporations have taught me several important lessons. The one that stands out above all others is this: Success in a management position takes more than a first-class resume. As most executive search consultants who work at the executive level will tell you, "All candidates look good on paper." However, a quick look at Corporate America reveals that, in almost every industry, today's leaders offer more than native smarts and specialized knowledge. They also demonstrate a strong grasp of business fundamentals and, most important, emotional intelligence.

Business Fundamentals

No senior executive with aspirations for the top job can afford to be without several meat-and-potatoes business skills and characteristics:

Exposure to corporate governance. Boardroom experience is a critical landmark on the development path of any executive aiming for a CEO role. Whether they serve on their own organization's board or another company's board, future leaders will deal with key issues like succession planning, business strategy, financial imperatives, the structure of executive compensation, and the role of shareholders.

Wall Street savvy.   To be seen as a top-level player in any organization, it's vital for executives to have exposure to Wall Street and the processes that shape a company's market valuation. Understanding the role of security analysts and the financial media, along with the ability to communicate performance expectations and answer hard questions about strategy and tactics are essential weapons in every top executive's arsenal of skills.

Strategic mindset.   Corporate America has produced many effective tacticians. However, the ability to think and manage *strategically* is what truly distinguishes leaders from managers. By building a vision of what businesses the organization should be and not be in, identifying its strengths and opportunities, positioning it effectively against competition, and structuring it to reach its maximum potential, strategists such as Bob Kidder (Borden), Harvey Golub (American Express), Lou Gerstner (IBM), Michael Jordan (CBS), and Chuck Lee (GTE) demonstrate the "vision thing" required of top leaders.

Profit and loss management.   A surprising number of top executives are uncomfortable reading a balance sheet or comparing net present values. Roberto Goizueta, CEO of Coca-Cola, was trained as a chemical engineer, but it was his ability to work with complex economic concepts that made him a hero to the company's shareholders. Core to all successful companies, accounting and finance enable an executive to understand, among other things, how the organization raises and allocates capital. It will also make clear why that new product the company has designed might not be launched, despite a sensational showing in test markets.

Marketing strategy and brand awareness.   Generating revenues is the fundamental principle of almost every private-sector organization. Even if their background is finance, research and development, or something else seemingly remote from marketing, today's leaders know how to target a market, capitalize on brand equity, and position a product. This knowledge helps to keep them focused on what should never be far from their minds: the customer.

Understanding the potential of information technology.   Knowing how information technology can be leveraged to achieve competitive advantage is essential for today's executive. Leaders must understand the role information systems play in shaping their current markets and operations, and in improving their business processes and performance. A warning, however: Don't become so preoccupied with technology that you lose sight of the big picture and the importance of human interaction. Charles Wong, CEO of Computer Associates, cautions that reliance on e-mail can depersonalize organizations and overwhelm managers with unnecessary detail. At his organization, e-mail is discouraged, and executives are expected to walk down the hall to communicate, person-to-person.

Defining Emotional Intelligence

There's more to successful leadership than a high IQ and an MBA. Emotional intelligence—knowing how to manage different personalities, when to trust a coworker with a confidence, and how to assess an organizational culture—is as vital to effective management as understanding internal rate of return or regression analysis. Emotional intelligence is what makes a leader a leader.

Emotional intelligence comprises five key dimensions:

- *People skills.*   Ability to relate to people in a variety of contexts.
- *Cultural sensitivity.*   Awareness of the unique traditions and behavior patterns that characterize the organization.
- *Intuition.*   Ability to make decisions in the midst of competing forces and uncertainty.
- *Perspective.*   Ability to understand how today's actions and decisions relate to the big picture and the downstream impact.
- *Stature.*   Emotional stability, social poise, and confidence.

Two recent examples illustrate how essential emotional intelligence is. In the first, a major technology company was evaluating two external candidates for its top executive position. Although both had impressive resumes, technical sophistication, and the ability to talk the game, it became clear that only one was able to rise above his "technical guru" role and relate successfully to nontechnical constituencies.

In contrast, Larry Weinbach, managing partner of Andersen Worldwide, was able to transcend his financial background by combining top-level financial savvy with a partnerlike approach to managing. Weinbach's effectiveness with colleagues as well as clients earned him the CEO slot at Unisys, whose market value has risen 150 percent since his arrival in 1997.

Executive search professionals have known for a long time that emotional intelligence is a critical element in executive hires. As companies begin to recognize this vital factor, they are beginning to analyze it more rigorously. Some actually screen for emotional intelligence using proprietary tests that gauge the compatibility of an executive's background, style, and personality with their organization. However, in our experience, the best way to predict future behavior is to learn about past behavior from colleagues, former employers, clients, and others who have worked with the candidate.

People Skills

You can't be in the executive search business long without realizing how important people skills are. Finance, accounting, information technology—almost any kind of intellectual skill—can be taught, for a price. People skills, however, are tougher, attacking otherwise smart, highly successful people. For example, Dick Snyder, former head of publishing giant Simon & Schuster, pushed the company to higher and higher earnings. However, according to many observers, he was disrespectful to subordinates. When Viacom acquired S&S, Frank Biondi, Viacom's CEO, fired Snyder.

Robert Lemire, a GE engineer, decided that what his company really needed was a department of creativity and innovation to solicit suggestions from employees. When his proposal was rejected by his superiors, he went to GE's annual meeting and volunteered his services as "a dumb lieutenant who will be able to tell CEO Jack Welch when he is naked." He failed to win election to the board but, undaunted, went back to his plant, where he circulated a poll, via office e-mail, to 5,400 employees, asking them to rate GE's employee innovation initiatives. GE appropriately pushed him out in the summer of 1994 for "a huge unauthorized use of e-mail."

Thanks to the weakening of corporate hierarchies, ours is the age of "horizontal structures" and competence-led decision teams. Nowadays, even intellectual stars must solicit help from others. They must learn how to persuade, listen, exercise patience and restraint, offer sympathy, feel empathy, and recover from the emotional assaults common to group give-and-take. I've seen scores of executives with superb technical expertise who neglected their people skills. No matter how brilliant they are, someone finally says, "You know, I don't care if Johnson is making twice his quota. He's a jerk. I want him out of here."

The good news is: Emotional intelligence can be learned, increased, and enhanced. One important aspect of it is optimism. Met Life, for example, tested salespeople for optimism, which predicts performance. Salespeople who scored high for optimism sold 37 percent more insurance than the pessimists. Optimist applicants who failed to meet Met Life's other standard test criteria were hired anyway. This group outsold its pessimistic counterparts by 21 percent its first year and by 57 percent the next. You'll be interested to know that optimism can be taught—there are books devoted to the subject.

Observational skills are another key competency. Researchers have devoted professional lifetimes to reading the cues and clues that signal what people are thinking and feeling. Most of us don't fully use our powers of observation. The way people gesture, the look in their eyes, the tone of their voice, the words they choose—all of these factors disclose how others feel and what they are thinking.

Cultural Sensitivity versus Restoring the Passion

Most experts believe an organization's culture is an amalgam of its values, operational behaviors, and attitudes toward change. More simply, corporate culture is "how we do things around here." When a company recruits a new CEO from the outside, it typically means that the organization's culture is in some way not supporting its vision and strategy. The new leader's challenge is to keep the best of the culture, root out unproductive processes, and infuse new behaviors and processes. That isn't easy. Beginning with a careful assessment of the current culture, new leaders must construct their program and, hardest of all, build support and excitement for it.

When Lou Gerstner took over at IBM, the company's inward focus, arrogance, and lack of competitiveness in a rapidly changing market were his initial targets. At the same time, he sought to preserve IBM's strong research and development function and its commitment to excellence. Similarly, Joe Clayton changed Frontier Communications to a marketing-driven, customer-oriented organization and accelerated product rollouts while keeping its technological development capabilities.

Although companies often try to change their cultures by hiring someone "new and different" from the outside, new executives won't accomplish much unless they recognize the organization's cultural patterns and the intractability of tradition. And their ability to frame change and generate excitement for it is paramount. Even the best-designed change effort may fail if the company does not gain significant buy-in from employees and other key constituencies.

Intuition Becomes Gut Instinct

Top executives must demonstrate unconditional commitment to their vision and have the self-confidence to inspire those who carry out the strategy. At the same time, they must be flexible enough to alter course if the evidence clearly demands it. The ability to make tough decisions without reacting or panicking is also a hallmark of top leaders. These skills are the most difficult to define and learn.

Management books recommend making decisions by looking at all the options, identifying the evaluation criteria, weighing the options numerically, and selecting the option with the highest score. Everybody talks about that approach. The fact is, hardly any executive ever uses it.

Since gut instinct enters into rational decision-making, experts have begun to wonder if it might not be harnessed to the decision-maker's advantage. How do army officers actually make decisions on the battlefield? Most of the time they size up a situation and do what gut instinct tells them— what we call intuition. But because we don't have a vocabulary for it, a lot of organizations don't trust it.

The Marine Corps tried to learn more about gut instinct through a novel experiment. For two days, 11 senior officers, including several generals, were assigned to the care of traders at the New York Mercantile Exchange. Why? Generals in time of war must analyze complex information quickly under high-stress conditions, making split-second decisions. Traders do that all the time, as they buy and sell and shout and scream at each other in the pits. Perhaps the traders could teach the generals a thing or two. So, after a little coaching (and after the exchange had closed for the evening), the generals began to trade.

It wasn't pretty. Real traders winced as their pretend counterparts yelled things to one another like, "Ten at $290, sir!" One general said to another condescendingly, "No, no. I'm the seller; you're the buyer." Slowly, however, they improved, and by session's end the guys with diamond studs in their ears were patting their charges on their olive-drab backs.

Analytical problem-solving is fine, if you have all the time in the world. But traders don't have time. Neither do most executives. If they have to stop to think about it, they lose millions of dollars. Their smartness lies in experience—as much relevant experience as they can get their hands on. It may not always be easy. Potential leaders need to build up experience quickly. To sharpen decision-making skills, forward-thinking professionals have rotated through a variety of jobs within their specialty and served on high-level project teams. They have soaked up as much second-hand experience as possible from oldtimers in the office. Most important, they anticipate the types of experience that will be needed tomorrow. If their organization is expanding to Mexico, they take a vacation south of the border.

Perspective

Top executives are always balancing scores of issues, projects, personalities, and outcomes. Understanding how each of them figures into the larger picture, the overall organization, the markets in which the company competes, and the impact of possible future trends is what separates the leaders from the led. The ability to think long-term is also a key element of perspective. A top executive's focus must extend far into the future—at least a decade, if not longer. As CEO of pharmaceutical giant Merck, Ray Gilmartin has a vision to build a world-class institution with global brand and identity. He has set a course that extends to the middle of the next century, considering many future possibilities, including new markets and new technology, and he stays it with quiet confidence.

The ability to focus is another key element of emotional intelligence. When recruiting top executives, we always look for candidates who see the big picture and focus on how to achieve their objectives. Leaders are rarely distractible: they focus on one issue at a time and give it 100 percent of their attention. They also see how one decision impacts other important strategic considerations. They lean forward slightly when they sit—a mark of attentiveness—and they listen carefully. When we interview candidates, we also look for well-developed communication skills and the ability to explain complex issues in simple language. Articulate executives get to the heart of the matter quickly and avoid larding their comments with jargon.

Stature and Charisma

A top executive must have stature, or social poise. The strongest executives understand that they are always on stage. They arrive on time and move crisply. They make the first move to shake hands—solidly. They are able to lead one or two minutes of initial small talk with ease. They periodically use the first names of others with whom they are interacting when making points, but not so much that they sound like salespeople. What they don't do is appear flustered or out of control.

An executive's charisma refers mainly to his or her ability to appear interested, caring, and concerned. Charlotte Beers, legendary CEO of Ogilvy & Mather, defines charisma as "wit, humor and the ability to express joy." Remembering names, cordiality, and empathy are all important. Charismatic executives usually like to have people around them and mention others in conversation. They walk the halls of their organization and chat easily with employees at all levels. Although it's difficult to assess charisma in a one-to-one interview, we look for subtle cues—like giving credit to team members and subordinates.

The evidence is indisputable: Professional accomplishments are not the only requirements for selecting a top executive. Now more than ever, the intangibles are what will ultimately land executives the job—no matter how good their credentials are. Scrutinizing a candidate's fundamentals and emotional intelligence is essential to determining whether he or she will thrive—or bomb—in a new environment.

INDEX

Acquisitions, 8, 70, 157, 158
Adaptability, 48, 71, 103
Advertising, 99, 104–106
Agency.Com, 80
Allen, Paul, 52
Allen, Robert, 90, 91
Amazon.com, 102, 105
American Association of Health Plans, 117
American College of Healthcare Executives, 117
American College of Physician Executives, 112, 117
American Organization of Nurse Executives, 114, 117
American Society for Healthcare Human Resources Administration (ASHHRA), 115, 117
America Online (AOL), 92, 102, 188
Analytical skill, 51, 53, 70, 72
Apple Computer, 187
Armstrong, C. Michael, 190
Association of Executive Search Consultants (AESC), 27, 28, 89
AT&T, 5, 90–93, 190

Barclay's Bank, 82
Barksdale, Jim, 93, 94
Beers, Charlotte, 234
Biondi, Frank, 230
Boeing, 79
Bonuses, 212–213
Boston Chicken, 185
Brunswick Corporation, 185
Business plans, 94
Business school, 67, 71, 80–81

Cahouet, Frank, 144
Career:
    assessing, 25
    continuity in, 5, 133, 152, 188
    life cycle of, 127

Career advancement, 40
    through cross-functionalism, 177–180
    in information technology jobs, 58, 63–64
    through the Internet, 61
    obstacles to, 8
    on Wall Street, 53–54
Career goals, 28, 40, 62, 129
    and company size, 129–130
    and cross-functionalism, 179
    personal fulfillment as, 110
    proactive approach to, 7, 63
Career opportunities:
    in entertainment/media field, 99–105
    evaluating, 209
    for future, 157
    in health care, 109–115
    in information technology, 58–59, 70
    in management consulting, 67–70
    nonadvancing, 28, 63, 131
    in publishing, 105–106
    on Wall Street, 47–54
    See also International opportunities
Career path, 224
    and cross-functionalism, 175–180
    for minorities, 153
    nontraditional, 141–142
    and teamwork, 177
Career strategy, 37
    and company size, 127–128
    nontraditional, 141–143
    and overseas assignments, 141, 166
    recruiter help with, 19
Career transition planning, 153–155
Casey, Al, 191
CFO magazine, 216
Change management, 5–8, 68
Changing companies, 5, 7, 8, 33
    in entertainment/media industry, 100

Changing companies (*Continued*):
　in information technology industry, 62
　and new employment contract, 188
　within small business, 131
　on Wall Street, 54
Changing functions. *See* Cross-functionalism
Changing industries, 141, 142, 185–191
　into entertainment/media, 101
　into health care, 116
　into information technology, 63
　into management consulting, 72, 190
　into publishing, 105
Changing jobs, 5–11, 37, 92
　lateral moves in, 28, 131, 166
　reasons for, 28
　timing of, 6, 19, 155, 191
　to Wall Street, 52–53
　See also Cross-functionalism; Job hunting
Charisma, 234
Chief executive officer (CEO):
　boardroom experience for, 227
　compensation packages for, 140, 210, 213–214
　and cross-functional moves, 178, 180
　and discretion in job searches, 33
　and employee retention, 61
　in health care industry, 109–111, 116
　and human resources responsibility, 144
　and information technology, 57
　and job offer negotiations, 199
　and minority job candidates, 151
　in new media industry, 103
　nontraditional, 142
　qualifications of, 227–234
　and senior management changes, 9
Chief financial officer (CFO), 109–110
　and compensation negotiation, 210
　and cross-functionalism, 51, 116, 178, 189
Chief information officer (CIO), 8
　cross-functionalism, 178
　in health career, 109, 112–113
Chief nurse executive (CNE), 114
Chief operating officer (COO), 39, 190–191
　and compensation negotiation, 210
Cisco, 62
Clayton, Joe, 231
Coca-Cola, 79, 82, 93, 190
Collaboration, 144, 145
Comcast, 99
Communication, 70, 143, 190, 233
　as competitive advantage, 60, 68
　for new hires, 222
　as Wall Street qualification, 50
Company culture:
　assessing, 229
　and CEO, 231–232
　family-friendliness in, 140
　fitting in with, 7, 27, 101, 128–129
　and human resources departments, 115
　and international markets, 82
　in "MBA Dream Companies," 70
　in small versus large companies, 126
　support in, 94, 129
Company size, 125–133
　and career path, 127–131

and compensation negotiation, 210
and job availability, 131–132
and leadership, 142
and training, 130
and work style, 128–129
Compensation, 28
　and at-will employment, 201–204
　in health careers, 110–111
　in Internet companies, 61
　and job satisfaction, 140
　negotiating, 198, 209–216
　perks, 214
　severance, 215
　stock options, 213–214
Compensation consultation, 215
Competition:
　and career advancement, 178
　global, 5
　and information technology, 58
　intercompany, 67
　for jobs, 8, 100
　for start-up ventures, 94
　on Wall Street, 48
Competitive advantage, 60, 68, 228–229
Compliance officer (CO), 113
CompuServe, 92, 102
Conferences, 10, 63, 116–117
Conflict management, 71
Consulting. *See* Compensation consultation; Management consulting
Continuing education, 152
Continuous quality improvement (CQI), 115, 118
Core competencies, 7, 68
Cortes, Felipe, 143
Creativity, 48, 71, 152
　and entrepreneurialism, 92
　in problem solving, 62
Cross-functionalism, 7, 50, 175–181, 187
Cultural fit, 128–129
Cultural sensitivity, 81–82
Customer service, 59, 60, 71, 103

D'Allesandro, David, 143
Decision-making, 232, 233
Delayering, 175
Denison, Susan, 103, 106
Deregulation, 186
Direct broadcast satellite (DBS), 103–104
Discrimination, 149, 150
Disney, 215
Distribution marketing, 59
Downsizing, 5, 67–68, 125, 129, 157
　and media senior management, 99–100
　of middle management, 186
　in publishing industry, 105
　and termination provisions, 200
Drug testing, 204

Eastman Kodak, 5
E-commerce, 57, 60, 61, 69
EDGAR (SEC web site), 29
Education:
　business school, 67, 71
　for global skills, 80–81

postgraduate, in health careers, 110
  See also MBA degree
Eldredge, Peter, 105
Electronic resume scanners, 41
E-mail, 57, 60, 158
  networking via, 63
  overreliance on, 229
  unauthorized use of, 230
Emotional intelligence, 186, 227, 229–234
Employee loyalty, 61, 101, 188
Employment contract, 188, 199–204, 215
English language, dominance of, 80
Enterprise transformation, 68
Entertainment/media industry, 99–106
  growth in, 157
  international opportunities in, 101–102
  transferring into, 101
  virtual companies in, 188
Entrepreneurialism, 89–95, 157
  in direct broadcast satellite market, 103–104
  international opportunities for, 59–60
  and the Internet, 92–93
  in small businesses, 125, 158
Entrepreneurial spirit, 51, 71, 103, 145
Ethnic cultures, 83
E*Trade, 102
Euro Market, 59
Executive Agenda, 73
Executive search. *See* Recruiters; Recruitment
Exit interview, 11
Expatriate managers, 83–84, 101–102, 163–170. *See also* International opportunities
Experience, 7, 52, 133, 233
  and compensation level, 212
  in health careers, 110, 111
  international, 59, 80, 85, 101
  in management consulting, 71
  in small versus large company, 126–129, 133
Extranet, 60

Family responsibilities, 28, 84, 140
Federal Express, 93
Fidelity Investments, 79
Financial management, 67, 70, 114, 228
Fisher, George, 190
Flattened organizations, 68, 157, 175, 188, 211, 230
  communication in, 143, 144
  See also Restructuring
Flexibility:
  in entrepreneurialism, 94
  and international marketplace, 82
  organizational, 175
  as personal asset, 7, 71, 100, 118, 152
  in small company, 132–133
Foreign languages, value of, 81, 141
Fortune best large companies to work for, 132
401(k), 191, 214
Frontier Communications, 231

Gates, Bill, 51, 99
General Electric, 8, 211, 230
Generalists, 152
General Motors, 163
Gerstner, Louis, 142, 190, 228, 231

Gilmartin, Ray, 233
Glass ceiling, 140
Global marketplace, 49, 79, 158
  and cross-functionalism, 176
  in entertainment/media industry, 101
  for executives, 140–141
  and information technology, 59–60
  for minorities, 159
Goizueta, Roberto, 190
Golub, Harvey, 190, 228
Greenspan, Alan, 80

Harreld, Bruce, 185
Healthcare Financial Management Association, 117
Health care industry, 109–119
  and management consulting, 70
  top positions in, 112–115
  transferring into, 116
Healthcare Information and Management Systems Society, 117
Herbold, Bob, 187
Hewlett-Packard, 62
Hiring manager, 37–41
Honesty:
  with recruiters, 20–21, 27
  on resume, 39
  in telephone contact, 38–39
Hughes Electronics, 190
Human resources, 38, 40, 144
  and cross-functionalism, 175–177, 179–180
  entertainment/media opportunities in, 101
  health care opportunities in, 111, 115
  and minority hiring, 149
  as transferable skill, 190
  and worker retention, 151
Hunt-Scanlon, 27–28

IBM, 62, 163
  and cross-industry hiring, 142, 185, 187
  dress code at, 30
  organizational changes at, 5, 231
Information technology (IT) industry, 57–64, 93, 176, 187
  career advancement in, 63–64
  and domestic opportunities, 60
  and international opportunities, 59–60
  as management consulting specialty, 67, 69–70
  and networking, 63
  as transferable skill, 189–190
  transferring into, 63
  understanding of, as CEO qualification, 228–229
Initiative, 145, 152
Innovation, 5, 67, 178
Integrated delivery systems (IDS), 109, 119
Integrity, 71, 118–119
Intel, 62, 163
Intellectual capital, 47, 48, 68, 72
Intellectual property, 11
International opportunities, 7, 59–60, 79–85, 141, 158–159
  in cable media, 104
  cultural sensitivity in, 81–82
  in entertainment/media industry, 101–102
  and executive postings, 163–170

International opportunities (*Continued*):
  and foreign language ability, 81
  management recruiting for, 100
  training for, 80–81
Internet, 57, 61, 80, 103, 116
  ad revenues for, 99
  and career opportunities, 58, 59, 61, 63, 100, 132
  and entrepreneurialism, 92–93
  hiring trends in, 102–103
  and information technology management, 60
  researching companies on, 26, 132
Internships, 52, 111
Interpersonal skills, 70, 144, 186, 229–231
Interviews, 25–33
  with client company, 31–33
  and confidentiality, 27, 29, 33
  final, 32–33
  for management consulting, 71
  and personal appearance, 29–31
  with recruiters, 26–28
  telephone screening, 9
  whom to meet in, 220, 223
Intranet, 60
Intuition, 229, 232–233

Job hunting, 6, 10, 38, 40
  and company size, 125–127
  for international position, 83
  pinpointing companies, 61–62
Job offers, 197–205
  and compensation package, 209–216
  as leverage with current employer, 198
  negotiating, 198–199
  See also Offer letter
Job satisfaction, 6, 7, 110, 140
Job security, 7–8, 198, 200, 201
  and company size, 130–131
Job skills:
  marketability of, 18, 25, 52, 156, 188–190
  in marketing, 59, 105
  upgrading, 7, 53, 64, 118, 152
John Hancock, 143
Johnson, Ned, 144
Johnson & Johnson, 185
Jordan, Michael, 190, 228

Kampouris, Mano, 142
Kelch, Anna, 104
Kidder, Bob, 228
Knowledge management, 68, 139, 187

Larson, Peter, 185
Leadership, 64, 71, 118, 138, 143, 157–158
  and emotional intelligence, 229
  grooming for, 180
  and international experience, 170
  for minority professionals, 158
Lee, Chuck, 228
Lemire, Robert, 230
Liability clause, in employment contract, 204

Magazines, 99, 103, 105–106
Malcom, John, 105
Managed care organizations (MCOs), 109, 111, 119

Management, 58–60. *See also* Financial management;
    Knowledge management; Middle management;
    Senior management
Management consulting, 67–75
  demand for, 67, 72
  and information technology, 69–70
  recruiting for, 71–73
  as transferable skill, 72, 190
Management information system (MIS), 59
Management services organization (MSO), 110, 119
Mandl, Alex, 89–92, 94
Manufacturing, 67, 187, 190
Marketing:
  background in, for CEO, 228
  career opportunities in, 59
  to international consumers, 82
  in publishing, 106
  as transferable skill, 102, 105, 189, 191
Market share, 7, 67
Market value of job skills, 18, 25
  in health care, 111
  maximizing, 52, 188–190
  in tight employment market, 156, 211
  on Wall Street, 49
Mastandrea, Pat, 100
MBA degree, 210
  for health career, 110, 112
  and international assignments, 81
  for management consulting, 71, 72
  for publishing career, 105
  in sports marketing, 106
  for Wall Street entry, 50
"MBA Dream Companies" (*Fortune*), 70
McCaw Cellular, 93
McDonald's, 79, 82
Medical foundation, 110, 119
Medical Group Management Association, 117
Mentoring, 40, 64, 118, 223–224
  among minority groups, 150–152
Merck, 233
Mergers, 5, 8, 157
  and functional transferability, 187–188
  international, 158
  and termination provisions, 200, 202
Merrill Lynch, 79
Metropolitan Life, 231
Microsoft, 52, 62, 92, 163, 187
Microsoft Expedia, 102
Middle management, 186, 211
  compensation packages for, 212
  minorities in, 150
Miller, Steve, 188
Minority job candidates, 149–159
Mitigation clause, in employment contract, 203–204
Money centers, major, 85
Multinational corporation (MNC), 163, 170

Nacchio, Joe, 214
National Association of Health Services Executives,
    117
National Black MBA Association (NBMBAA), 156
National Business Employment Weekly, 99
National Managed Health Care Congress, 117
Negotiation, of job offer, 197–205

for compensation package, 209–216
   and termination provisions, 200–202
Netscape, 92, 93
Networking, 37, 40, 63, 116–117, 151
   in entertainment/media industry, 106
   in industry associations, 10
   among minority groups, 150, 155–156
   "old boys," 49
   with recruiters, 9–10, 16, 17
   for Wall Street jobs, 53
Noncompete restrictions, 203, 204

Observational skills, 231
Offer letter, 200–204
Office politics, 221, 223–224
Ohga, Noria, 145
"Old boy" network, 49, 151
Operations, 67
Oracle, 163
O'Rourke, J. Tracy, 139
"Out of the box" recruiting, 100, 142
Outplacement, 6
Outsourcing, 6, 59, 129, 150
Ovitz, Michael, 215

Peer equity issues, 18
Pepsico, 82, 163, 187
Performance, 7
   and bonuses, 213
   evaluation of, 70, 153, 154
   in management consulting, 73–74
Perks, 214
Personal appearance, 29–31
Perspective, in leadership, 229, 233
Persuasion, 50, 71
Physician executives, 112
Physician Executives' Survey, 112, 113, 118
Physician practice management companies
      (PPMCs), 109, 111, 115, 119
Pittman, Bob, 188
Problem solving, 54, 71, 72, 233
Prodigy, 92
Product development, 189
Productivity, 6, 57, 73
Product manager, 59
Product marketing, opportunities abroad, 59, 82
Professionalism, 30, 39
Profit sharing, 214
Project management, 58, 71, 129
Proprietary information, 27, 203
Publishing, 105–106

Quality, management programs for, 115
Qwest Communications International, 214

Recession, 6, 176
Recruiters:
   honesty with, 20–21, 27
   initiating contact with, 19–20, 38
   interviews with, 26–28
   in negotiation, 199, 215–216
   and niche technology, 90
   recommendations to, 10, 17
   relationship with, 16, 19, 25, 37, 40

Recruitment, 6–11, 211–212
   confidentiality in, 33
   cross-industry, 186–187
   in entertainment/media industry, 100, 105, 106
   of health care executives, 112
   for information technology jobs, 63
   for management consulting, 71
   of middle managers, 211
   of minority candidates, 150
   and networking, 9–10, 19
   "out of the box," 100, 142
   and small companies, 131–132
Reengineering, 68, 125, 150, 175, 186, 188
Referrals, to recruiters, 17, 31, 39
Relationships:
   cultural barriers in, 81
   with former employers, 155
   in management consulting, 70–71
   among minority professionals, 152, 156
   for new hires, 219–224
   within organizations, 68
   with recruiters, 16–19, 25, 37, 40
   on Wall Street, 49
   See also Mentoring; Networking
Relocation, 28, 131
   abroad, 82, 84
   expenses of, 214
   See also International opportunities
Reputation, 39, 64, 106
Research:
   on companies, 26, 29, 132, 154
   for start-up ventures, 94
Resigning, 11
Restructuring, 6, 32, 67–68, 211
   effect on minority hiring, 150
Resume, 38, 39
   electronic scanners for, 41
   maintaining current, 9, 26, 155
   for moving from small to large company, 133
Revenue generating, 189
   in advertising, 99
   as CEO qualification, 228
   on Wall Street, 50–53
Rightsizing, 175
Risk taking, 118
   and company size, 126, 130
   in entertainment/media industry, 101
   in entrepreneurialism, 91, 92, 131
   in Internet industry, 103
   in job hunting, 62
   in Wall Street career, 54
Rosso, Jean-Pierre, 142

Sculley, John, 187
Sea-Land Services, 90
Securities and Exchange Commission (SEC):
   compensation disclosure forms, 210
   web site (EDGAR), 29
Self-assessment, 25, 79, 191
Self-development strategy, 151–153
Self-promotion, 63–64
Seminars, 10, 40, 130, 220
Senior management:
   and compensation negotiation, 210, 212, 213

Senior management (*Continued*):
  and cross-functionalism, 175, 177–180, 185, 190
  in entertainment/media industry, 99
  and global enterprises, 163, 170
  in health care industry, 109–115
  hiring process for, 32
  international experience for, 80
  minorities in, 150, 157
  relationships with, 224
  and resignation with cause, 202
  turnover in, 5, 9
Severance packages, 215
Shareholders, 67
  employees as, 213–214
  improving value for, 48, 68, 74
"Silicon Alley" (New York), 102–103
Silicon Valley, 57, 60, 93
Simon & Schuster, 230
Small business, 125–127
Small Business Administration (SBA), 127, 132
Snyder, Dick, 230
Specialization:
  in advertising, 104
  and company size, 129–130
  functional, 185–186
  within management consulting, 67, 68
  in media management, 100
  on Wall Street, 50–53
Sports industry, 106, 151, 199
Start-up ventures, 91–95
  international, 158
  and the Internet, 103
  job security in, 131
  management recruiting for, 100
  See also Entrepreneurialism
Stature, in leadership, 229, 234
Stock options, in compensation packages, 213–214
Stock valuation, and CEO selection, 142
Strategic thinking, 118, 158
  as CEO qualification, 228
  as consulting specialty, 67, 70
Success, 33, 68
  changing nature of, for businesses, 175
  in health care career, 117–119
  organizational versus individual, 145
  qualities needed for, 138–139, 227
  on Wall Street, 48, 50, 51
Succession planning, 180, 227
Sun Microsystems, 92, 163
Synergy, 144

Talent pool, 71–73
  cross-functional, 179
  for Internet jobs, 102–103

Teamwork, 68, 70, 144–145
  for new hire, 222, 224
  project-based, 176–177
  rewards of, 75
  as work style, 128
Technological innovation, 5, 58, 60
  and entertainment/media, impact on, 99, 102, 104
  and entrepreneurial opportunity, 93
  and organizational flexibility, 175, 189–190
  overenthusiasm for, 143–144
Telecommunications, 58, 186, 187
  entrepreneurialism in, 91
  as management consulting specialty, 70
Teligent, 89–92
Termination, 200–204
Total quality management (TQM), 115, 118
Trade associations:
  for health care professionals, 117
  networking in, 10, 37, 39, 118, 156
Trade publications:
  as information source, 117
  writing for, 10, 40–41
Transferability. *See* Changing industries
Turnaround business experience, 7, 187, 222

Unemployment rate, 7, 186, 211
UniLever, 163
Unisys, 230

Value propositions, 68
Values, organizational, 27
Viacom, 100, 230
Virtual companies, 188
Visibility:
  maintaining, 10, 37, 40–41, 118, 155
  and overseas assignments, 141
Voice mail, evading, 38

Wall Street, 47–54
  attributes needed for, 51–52
  credentials for, 50, 52
  exposure to, for CEOs, 228
  and specialization, 50–53
Wal-Mart, 79
Web sites, 102, 106
Weinbach, Larry, 229
Welch, Jack, 139, 144, 190, 230
Willes, Mark, 189
Wong, Charles, 229
Workaholics, 139–140
Work style, 128–129

Yahoo, 92
Year 2000 problem, 69, 137